INCREASING YOUR
PLAY THERAPY
TOOL BOX

A collection of Play Therapy and Expressive Arts Interventions

Edited By Carmen Jimenez-Pride

Contributors: Angel Onley-Livingston, Alisia Mitchell, Sabra Starnes

ISBN-13: 978-0-692-04330-1
ISBN-10: 0-692-043306
Library of Congress: 9780692043301

Acknowledgment from the Editor

This book of tools is the first published play therapy resource developed by a group of all African American, licensed mental health providers and registered play therapists. My goal for this project was to bring a group of African American play therapy professionals with various training and experiences to strengthen the visibility of Play Therapists of Color.

Special thanks to the contributors: Angel, Alisha and Sabra your dedication to this project was amazing. I am looking forward great things in the future. We all bring variety and creativity to the field of counseling, social work and play therapy.

Special thanks to all the social workers, counselors, clinical professionals, Registered Play Therapists and other helping professionals who are dedicated to the wellbeing of children.

Special thanks to my amazing family, Fernanda Jimenez, Natalie Pride and Nathan Pride for their ongoing support and encouragement.

About the Editor

Carmen K. Jimenez-Pride is a Master Level Social Worker, Substance Abuse Professional, Licensed Clinical Social Worker in North Carolina and Georgia. She is also a Licensed Independent Social Worker in South Carolina.

Carmen is a Registered Play Therapist Supervisor credentialed by the Association of Play Therapy. She earned a Bachelor of Social Work with a certificate in Child Protective Services from Benedict College in 2004. She was accepted into the advance standing program at the University of South Carolina earning a Master of Social Work in 2005 with a focus on communities and organizations.

Carmen has over 20 years of experience in the mental health field. In 2011, She created Outspoken Counseling and Consulting to provide therapy, life coaching and business consulting in Fort Mill, South Carolina. In 2014, She transitioned the practice to Columbia, South Carolina. In 2016, she became a Registered Yoga Teacher and created freedOM Yoga Inc. an organization focused on providing yoga therapy services to individuals who normally would not have access to the practice of yoga.

In 2018, Carmen became a Registered Children Yoga Teacher. With a focus on children and play therapy Carmen is the founder of Play Therapy with Carmen Inc. an organization dedicated to educating the mental health community on play therapy and providing supervision, training and resources for licensed professionals.

Carmen is a past member of the North Carolina National Association of Social Work board of directors and North Carolina Association for Play Therapy board of directors. She is a current, and active member of the South Carolina Association of Play Therapy board of directors and the South Carolina Chapter of the National Association of Social Workers. Carmen is an adjunct professor at the University of South Carolina School of Social Work.

July 2017, Carmen published, No, No Elizabeth her first publication and first book in the Elizabeth the Adventure series. March 2019, Elizabeth Makes A Friend was published.

Carmen is the creator of Focus on Feeling© a play therapy curriculum focused on social and emotional development.

Carmen is a co-author of "Fiercely Speaking" published in 2019.

In addition, she has created and published a collection entitled "The Paper Personal Assistant", a collection of resources and guides for professionals.

About the Contributors

Rev. Angel Onley-Livingston, NCC, LPC, PEAT, SEAT

Angel is the owner and counselor at Mind Soul Spirit Professional Counseling Services DBA House of Abba LLC, which just broke through the 6-figure earning ceiling! How exciting for the "Soul Healing Coach". Angel obtained her B.A. in Interdisciplinary Studies with a focus in Early Childhood Education and Psychology in 2004. A Master of Arts with an emphasis of Mental Health from Webster University in 2006 and has completed 1 year of Seminary of the Master of Arts in Religion while at Lutheran Theological Southern Seminary, now Lenoir Rhyne. Angel also has two Doctoral classes under her belt from Walden University.

Angel's gregarious personality has afforded her the opportunity to be featured on FOX, WBTW, 98.5 KISS FM, Whitmore Alumni Magazine, and SC Woman Magazine. She is an Ordained Preacher, National Certified Counselor, Licensed Professional Counselor, Author, Spiritual Life Coach, Empowerment Speaker, and a Prophetic Voice. Angel's specialty is helping people heal the wounds of their soul. She has a spiritual gift that lets her discern the deep-rooted issues and she helps people heal them through counseling, spiritual life coaching, expressive arts skills, sand play and sand tray skills, play therapeutic skills, and her newest adventure, is The Soul Joy Gathering that is like a talk show and a meeting with your best friends all at one time. Angel is the Wife of Kevin Livingston and the mother of three loving protecting arrows (boys) Jabari (15) Kingston (6) Logan (5).

About the Contributors

Alisia Mitchell, MSW, LMSW

Alisia Mitchell is a licensed therapist serving children and families providing individual and family therapy, in the Prince George's County, MD area. Alisia attended the University of North Carolina at Greensboro receiving her bachelor's degree in Social Work with a minor in Sociology. While attaining her degree Alisia was able to travel to Costa Rica volunteering to serve at risk children in rural schools and helping to build beds for families in need.

After graduating, Alisia received the Child Welfare Collaborative Scholarship to work in a Department of Social Services for two years serving foster care children and youth. While facilitating social and life skills groups for children and adolescents in foster care, Alisia also became certified, "Making Proud Choices" sexual education facilitator for adolescents in foster care. With an overwhelming desire of supporting children to believe, feel capable, and trust in themselves encouraged the pursuance of attaining a master's degree in social work at Howard University, concentrating on Child Welfare.

While attending Howard University, Alisia became a graduate assistant gathering research on Hispanic/Latino families and domestic violence and other related material for faculty. After graduate school, Alisia found herself conducting more small groups of children age's 4-7 teaching children coping skills, peer conflict, and expressing self. Alisia plans to pursue more educational opportunities of research focusing on childhood trauma to develop unique play therapeutic interventions. Passionate about the mental health and well-being of children, Alisia's personal vision is, "Every child will have an opportunity to voice their life story in a safe environment and be heard."

About the Contributors

Sabra Starnes, MSW, LCSW, RPT-S

Sabra D. Starnes is a licensed clinical social worker in Maryland and Washington, DC. She has worked as a clinical social worker in the Washington, DC area, for over 20 years in various settings, hospitals, adoption agencies, schools, daycares, outpatient clinics and inpatient treatment centers.

Sabra has a Masters in Social Work from Catholic University and a Master's in Education from American University. She has her certification in Life Crisis Skills, Sand Tray, Play Therapy, Trauma, Loss and Grief. She is a Parenting the Love and Logic Way expert. She specializes in adoption, foster care, parenting issues and skills. She is very knowledgeable on support resources in the DMV, and often provides guidance to those needing immediate support. As a lifelong learner, she enjoys attending trainings, workshops and self-guided learning on new skills and techniques to enhance her clinical work with children, adults, families and couples.

Sabra is the owner and psychotherapist of Next Place Therapy, a small private practice, with offices in Maryland and Washington, D.C. She has owned her own business since 2001. They provide individual group and family therapy to children, couples and families. They also offer monthly parenting workshops and support groups to parents on such topics as balancing parenting and life, how to communicate and listen effectively to your children, helping young adults launch into the world, safety and the internet, understanding mental illness, loss and grief, and divorce. She has done workshops for children, families and adults on diversity, LGBTQ, growth and development, drug and alcohol prevention, warning signs of depression and other mental illness. Sabra supervises and trains mental health professionals on areas of child social emotional development, adoption and foster care, navigating the school system, and helping parents understand their child's IEP or 504.

Sabra is an active member in her community. She is instrumental in providing support on pressing issues in our community today. She is very passionate about working with youths and families at risk. She provides pro bono counseling to those who are unable to pay for therapy through the Pro Bono Counseling Project. She has served on various boards in the community.

In her personal life, Sabra is an adoptive mother of two sons, a wife, new grandma and someone who loves to live life to the fullest by traveling, spending time with family and friends, enjoying the outdoors. She enjoys swimming, bike riding, hiking, yoga and meditating.

Tool Box Activities

String of Hearts .... Sabra Starnes **3**

Mindfulness Jar .... Carmen Jimenez-Pride **5**

Hide and Go Seek my Feelings .... Alisia Mitchell **7**

Self-Awareness Self Portrait .... Angel Onley-Livingston **11**

Mixed up Feelings Shake Up .... Sabra Starnes **13**

Not your Normal Family Tree .... Carmen Jimenez-Pride **16**

I am in Control of my Feelings .... Alisia Mitchell **19**

Mind Game .... Angel Onley-Livingston **22**

Let your Feelings Out .... Sabra Starnes **24**

Empower Me .... Carmen Jimenez-Pride **26**

Musical Chairs with a Twist .... Alisia Mitchell **29**

Coping Skills Tool Kit .... Carmen Jimenez-Pride **31**

My Wheel of Emotions .... Alisia Mitchell **33**

Goals of the Week .... Carmen Jimenez-Pride **36**

Sculpting Clay Activity .... Angel Onley-Livingston **38**

Value Sticks .... Sabra Starnes **40**

Together We'll Grow .... Carmen Jimenez-Pride **43**

Communal Sand Tray .... Angel Onley-Livingston **45**

Communal Sand Tray Villain & Hero .... Angel Onley-Livingston **47**

Rolling out my feelings........................... Alisia Mitchell **49**

Check me, Check you .... Sabra Starnes **53**

Marble Jar Friends .... Sabra Starnes **57**

Using Your Brain Power .... Sabra Starnes **60**

Help! I'm Feeling Puzzled .... Alisia Mitchell **63**

Learning About My Feelings .... Carmen Jimenez-Pride **66**

A Letter to A Parent Who's in Prison .... Angel Onley-Livingston **69**

What I wish For You .... Sabra Starnes **71**

I Am a Gift, You Are a Gift .... Alisia Mitchell **73**

Dear John, Dear Jane .... Carmen Jimenez-Pride **76**

Teamwork Makes the Dream Work .... Angel Onley-Livingston **78**

Hopes, Wishes and Dreams........................... Sabra Starnes **80**

My Safety Circle... Alisia Mitchell **82**

Feelings Comic Strips .... Angel Onley-Livingston **85**

Show How Great You Are .... Sabra Starnes **88**

Pathway to my Feelings .... Alisia Mitchell **91**

Feelings Scale .... Carmen Jimenez-Pride **94**

Super Hero Video .... Angel Onley-Livingston **96**

Affirmations in the Sand .... Sabra Starnes **98**

Think Before I Speak .... Carmen Jimenez-Pride **101**

This is my Story................................... Alisia Mitchell **104**

Family Crest .... Angel Onley-Livingston **107**

Negative and Positive Thoughts Memory Game .... Sabra Starnes **109**

End of the Rainbow .... Carmen Jimenez-Pride **112**

Personal Crest Collage .... Angel Onley-Livingston **114**

Doll Making Activity .... Angel Onley-Livingston **116**

String of Hearts

Contributed By: Sabra Starnes

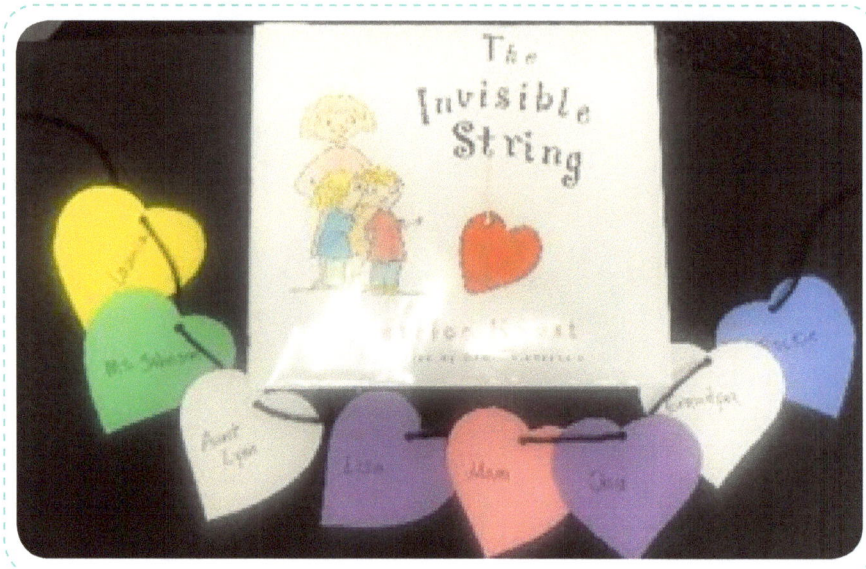

- ○ **Treatment Modality : Family**
- ○ **Treatment Phase: Engagement**

Materials Needed

1 **Book:** The Invisible -String by Patrice Karst (A live recording can be found on YouTube.)
2 **String**
3 **Colored construction paper**
4 **Scissors**
5 **Markers**

Goal of the activity

To help clients express their feelings of sadness, fear, worry, loss and grief around a person who is no longer in their lives due to death, separation, foster care or adoption.

Activity Steps

○ **Step 1**

+ The family or therapist reads the story.

+ During the story, stop and have a brief discussion with the family to make the story relevant to what they are dealing with.

○ **Step 2**

+ After reading the story have the family draw and cut out hearts. Label each heart with the names of the family member or loved ones and connect hearts with string. The family decides where they want their hearts of string to go to remember loved ones.

Discussion

This is a great initial activity to do with a family to discuss how to support the client who may be dealing with separation and anxiety, loss and grief of family members, friends or special people to the child and or family.

This bibliotherapy book helps clients to be able to make their own connections relate to the topics of separation and anxiety and loss and grief. The book and activity can help the child be able to process their own thoughts and feelings of loss, worries and sadness around someone who is no longer in their life.

Mindfulness Jar

Contributed By: Carmen Jimenez-Pride

- Treatment Modality: Individual, Family
- Treatment Phase: Working

Materials Needed

1. **Mason jar** (any jar or bottle with a tight lid)
2. **Glitter, plastic confetti**
3. **Clear glue**
4. **Food coloring (optional)**

Goal of the activity

Create a mindfulness resource with multiple uses.

Activity Steps

o **Step 1**

+ Fill jar/bottle half way with warm water.

o **Step 2**

+ Add clear glue.

o **Step 3**

+ Add more water, filling 1 inch from top.

o **Step 4**

+ Add glitter, plastic confetti materials.

o **Step 5**

+ Close lid tight (you can use a strong glue to seal the top).

o **Step 6**

+ Shake until glue and glitter is mixed well.

Discussion

The more glue added to the jar the slower the glitter will fall. Allowing the child to participate in as many activity steps as possible will ensure the child becomes vested in the jar and presented activity. When doing a family focused activity give the child directives and allow the child to then take lead by sharing what to do next with the other individuals in the session. Jars can be left in the office or given to the child to take home.

Mindfulness activities can include using the jar to refocus thoughts when having increased feelings of anger, fear or anxiety. The jars are an excellent tool for teaching breathings techniques. As the jar materials settle, individuals are encouraged to engage in deep inhales through the nose and exhales through the mouth to bring calmness to the body while visually focused on the items inside the jar.

Jars can be used in session as a timekeeper when doing journal activities and thinking activities. Utilizing the jars within the home setting can be used as a time-in method instead of a parent putting the child in time-out. Encouraging the child to focus on the colors and as they fall to the bottom of the jar. To further increase the investment in the jar, have the child and parent identify ways they can utilize the jar within their environments.

Hide and Go seek my feelings

Contributed By: Alisia Mitchell

- Treatment Modality: Individual, Family
- Treatment Phase: Engagement, Working

Materials Needed

1. **Colored cotton balls**
2. **Plastic googly eyes**
3. **Three or more popsicle sticks**
4. **Glue**
5. **Permanent marker**

Goals of the activity

Supporting client or client/client's parent(s) to identifying feelings, building trust, and fostering bonding

Activity Steps

If choosing to create the feeling popsicle sticks prior to session:

o **Step 1**

+ Prepare by gluing the cotton balls and eyes to the popsicle sticks. Keep in mind the colored cotton balls/popsicle sticks represent different feelings (happy-yellow, sad-blue, angry-red, etc.).

o **Step 2**

+ Write the name of the feeling on the front or back of the popsicle stick. This can assist the child to identify the feeling with words.

If choosing to create the feeling popsicle sticks with the client and/or client's parent:

o **Step 1**

+ Prepare by having all material out for easy access for client and/or client's parent.

o **Step 2**

+ Introduce activity, "Today we will be playing a game about feelings. First let's work together in creating our feeling popsicle sticks." Therapist can facilitate a discussion to help client/client's parent in assigning colors to the feelings popsicle sticks. For example, therapist can say, "I wonder what feeling we could choose for the yellow popsicle stick?" Then allow client to answer.

o **Step 3**

+ Introduce activity, "Today we will be playing a game about feelings. First let's work together in creating our feeling popsicle sticks." Therapist can facilitate a discussion to help client/client's parent in assigning colors to the feelings popsicle sticks. For example, therapist can say, "I wonder what feeling we could choose for the yellow popsicle stick?" Then allow client to answer.

Step 4

After the popsicle sticks have been created the game can begin.

This game follows the rules as the original version of "Hide and Seek."

o **Step 1**

+ Therapist will say, "Now that we have created our feeling sticks we will play, "Hide and seek my feelings."

o **Step 2**

+ Explain to the client/client's parent one person will hide the popsicle sticks while the other close their eyes (be sure to give the child alternatives if they do not feel comfortable closing their eyes) to count to ten. Once the popsicle sticks are hidden the client/client's parent will try to find them. The therapist or parent will assist the child in naming what feeling they have located. client/client's parent can take turns hiding and seeking.

For children 6 and above:

o **Step 1**

+ After the feeling popsicle sticks have been created the therapist can support client/client's parent in understanding, "We all have feelings, but sometimes we hide our feelings. When we hide our feelings, others will not know how to help us. This game called, Hide and seek my feelings, helps us talks about our emotions."

o **Step 2**

+ Follow the same rules in step 2 in the above section for children ages 4-6.

o **Step 3**

+ Once the child finds the feelings, the therapist can ask the child to talk about a time they felt that emotion. Child and therapist can take turns in hiding and seeking feelings, and talking about a time they felt the emotion.

Important

While playing the game with child: It is recommended the therapist be mindful of their personal surroundings and "pretend" (Cover one hand on face allowing one eye open or turn sideways covering one eye) to pay attention to the child's movement and to keep the space protected.

Discussion

Many times, we experience children having trouble verbalizing their emotions, consequently some children repress or avoid their feelings. Additionally, we may encounter insecure or lack of attachment between a parent and child. For younger children, this activity encourages children to note how they are feeling, and supports bonding in a safe space for child and parent to express emotion, while parent simply listens without questioning the experience of the feeling. For older children, this activity assists teaching the importance of identifying and verbalizing their emotions safely to a trusted adult instead of avoiding or repressing.

Self-Awareness Self Portrait

Contributed By: Angel Onley-Livingston

○ **Treatment Modality: Individual, Group, Family**
○ **Treatment Phase: Engagement, Working, Termination**

Materials Needed

1. **Markers**
2. **Crayons**
3. **Colored Pencils**
4. **Poster Board/ newspaper print**
5. **Photos of child demonstrating emotions/or a mirror**

Goals of the activity

To explore emotions of anger, sadness, anxiety, fear, and happiness. Explore how the child processes emotions internally and how they project emotions outwardly towards the world. To gain personal awareness of inner emotions, internal impressions vs. universal thoughts, and internal conflicts.

Activity Steps

○ Step 1

+ Therapist will direct child use a pencil to sketch an image of themselves using a picture they have brought in from home, or allow child to take a picture using their cell phone. Provide a mirror for child to use to act out or to view themselves expressing emotions mentioned above.

○ Step 2

+ Therapist will direct the child to use art supplies, to draw a self-portrait demonstrating how client views themselves. The child can choose to draw one portrait or several portraits of themselves.

+ Therapist is recommended to remind the child the activity is not about skill level of drawing it is not right or wrong. Explain the activity is focused on what they see when they see themselves and feel these feelings.

Discussion

How do emotions of anger, sadness, anxiety, fear, and happiness show up for them in their personal lives, and how they project that image on the world? Therapist is recommended to discuss how child feels about themselves, what they like or wish to change or don't like about themselves. Explain the meaning of self-esteem and self-awareness.

With this activity a therapist can engage the child in a discussion on how they see themselves vs. how they feel they show up in the world?

Mixed up Feelings Shake Up

Contributed By: Sabra Starnes

○ **Treatment Modality: Individual**
○ **Treatment Phase: Engagement**

Materials Needed

1 **Book:** Double Dip Feelings by Barbra Cain
2 **4 different food colorings**
3 **An empty water bottle with lid**
4 **Baby oil**
5 **Spoon**
6 **Plastic cup**

Goals of the activity

To help the client understand that they can have different feelings about a situation or event and learn how to express themselves utilizing creative arts.

Activity Steps

○ **Step 1**

+ Therapist will read "Double Dip Feelings" and discuss the different experiences presented in the book.

○ **Step 2**

+ Therapist will engage the child in a visual expressive art activity by labeling the 4 colors a feeling, such as happy, mad, sad and scared.

○ **Step 3**

+ The therapist will prompt the child to pick a situation they have faced that led them to have two different feelings. (If the child has a hard time coming up with identifying a situation where they had 2 different feeling the child can choose a situation in the book).

○ **Step 4**

+ The therapist will prompt the child to pick the two colors that they identified to match their feelings.

○ **Step 4**

+ Therapist will assist the child with filling the bottle half with water and then adding one of their identified colors. With the lid on they will shake the bottle. (Turning the water, the identified color).

+ Next, in a separate cup the therapist will assist the child with pouring baby oil in the 2nd cup (the amount of baby oil should halfway fill the bottle). Therapist will assist the child in putting the second color into the baby oil and mix.

+ Finally, the colored baby oil is poured into the bottle with the colored water. When the bottle sits the colors are separated. The therapist will prompt the child to shake the bottle to mix the colors. This will give the child a visual of the colors can be mixed. The therapist will relate the colors to their feelings and the bottle to the identified situation.

This is an activity that can be done at the initial phase of treatment with individuals to help them work on expressing feelings and expressing having 2 different feelings about the same situation or event. Utilizing the bibliotherapy resource and creating a visual will give the child an opportunity to develop an understanding that they can have two feelings about a situation.

Ongoing discussion and the use of the created visual will help the child increase their verbal expression of thoughts and feelings.

Not Your Normal Family Tree

Contributed By: Carmen Jimenez-Pride

○ **Treatment Modality: Individual**
○ **Treatment Phase: Engagement**

Materials Needed

1. **Sand tray**
2. **Various miniatures**

Goals of the activity

The goal is to step away from the traditional genogram family connection methods and allow children to give you a visual of their views of family members and individuals in their support system.

Activity Steps

o Step 1

+ Therapist will allow the child to spend some time in the sand without any miniatures and explain the activity, utilize this time as a mindfulness practice. (telling the child to focus on their breath and the feel of the sand).

+ Take the time and explain that you would like to get to the know the important people in the child's life.

o Step 2

+ Allow the child to choose miniatures to identify members of their family and support system.

+ Once the child has chosen the miniatures direct the child to place them in the tray.

o Step 3

+ Allow the child to introduce you to their family. Depending on the age of the child, once they introduce you to the family member say, "nice to meet you". Be aware of the placement of the family members and document what miniature is used for each member of the family.

+ Allow the child as much time needed to introduce you to the family member. If the child has issues with talking about the family members, asking basic questions will help with engagement such as: "tell me some things you like to do with that family member" or "tell me some things that makes you smile about that family member" are some examples. If the child is not ready to share their family members take a picture or draw the positions to follow up with the child at a different time.

+ Taking pictures is a great way to assure you remember the placement and miniatures used. This activity can be repeated to evaluate changes in the family relationships, and dynamics.

Discussion

Sandtray therapy is a full sensory experience. A child can have a conscious and unconscious mind that are often in conflict. Sandtray therapy can integrate these two minds and help find resolutions to these internal conflicts. Children communicate through play and the toys are their words, so sandtray is an appropriate for children to express what is troubling them. The right brain is filled with images, creativity, and playfulness. We need to access the right brain for the healing to occur.

If you do not have traditional sand tray set up, you can use any type of container. This activity is perfect to use with a traveling sand tray container.

If you are looking for sand trays or items visit:

https://www.playtherapysupply.com/?tracking=5b89dd082307d

I am in Control of my Feelings

Contributed By: Alisia Mitchell

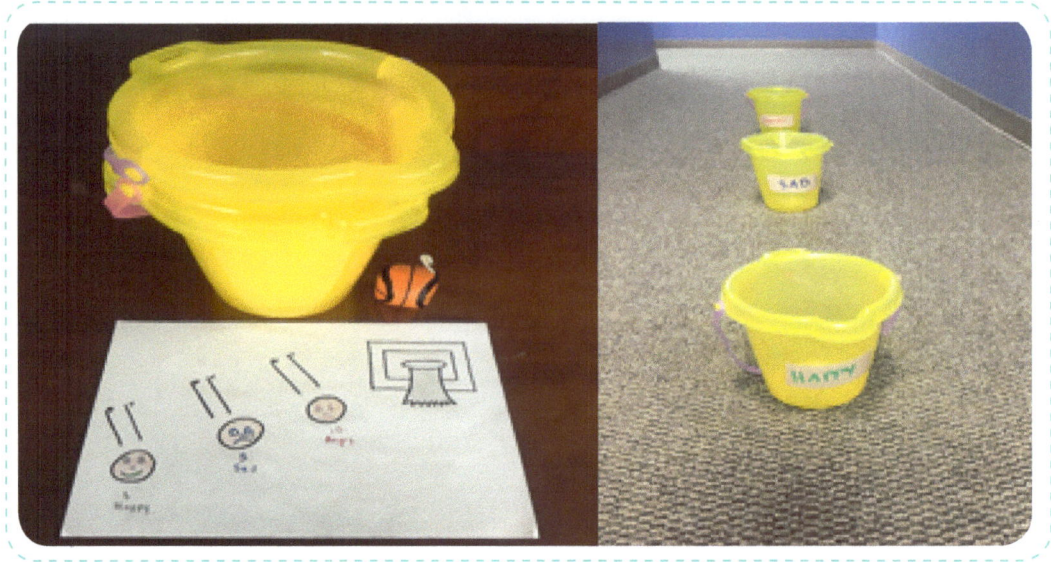

○ **Treatment Modality: Individual, Family**
○ **Treatment Phase: Engagement**

Materials Needed

1 **3-4 buckets**

2 **Small ball**

3 **Plain sheet of paper**

4 **Markers/colored pencils**

5 **Duct Tape**

6 **Permanent markers (optional)**

Goals of the activity

To identify feelings and appropriate coping skills to regulate/control emotions.

Activity Steps

Therapist will prepare prior to session:

○ Step 1

+ Using a pencil draw 3-4 medium-sized circles diagonally leading up toward a basketball goal. The basketball goal can be drawn by therapist or found online (i.e. browsing a clipart basketball goal). Please note, therapist will draw facial expressions inside the circles, which will be discussed in Step 4.

○ Step 2

+ Each circle represents how many points can be scored. For example, the first circle can be worth 1 point, second circle 5 points, and third circle 10 points. Therapist can choose the allotted points (i.e. 2, 4, 6, etc.).

○ Step 3

+ Write different feelings underneath each number/point. It is recommended to begin with an emotion child feels safe in expressing, such as "happy," then other challenging emotions.

○ Step 4

+ Once the feelings have been written, draw facial expressions representing each emotion inside the circles.

○ Step 5

+ Once the feelings have been written, draw facial expressions representing each emotion inside the circles.

○ Step 6

+ After all, has been drawn, therapist can use markers and pencils to emphasize drawings. It is recommended to assign colors to feelings, such as happy is green, blue is sad, red is angry.

Activity Steps for buckets:

The buckets are the "basketball goals." Place the buckets 2-4 feet apart from each other. Label each bucket with the selected feelings chosen in step 3 above (first bucket is happy, second bucket is sad, etc.), using duct tape and permanent markers. If choosing to omit labeling the buckets, it is important client is aware what each bucket represents and the feeling associated.

○ Step 1

+ Therapist will have the picture drawn in front of the child and parent as a visual while explaining the game.

○ Step 2

+ Therapist will begin, "We will play a game about our feelings and learn how to be more in control. The first goal is happy, the second goal is sad, and the third goal is angry. You will be in control of which bucket the ball is thrown into for points. You will stand at least 1 foot in front of all the buckets. Each goal you make we will discuss a time you felt that emotion. Then we will name two things to help control how you are feeling the next time."

+ **Therapist will write the coping skills (i.e. take a deep breath, blow bubbles, talk to a parent) on the two blank lines written above the facial expression. Therapist can determine if parent can participate to support client in creating the coping skills and motivating client to "make a goal."

Discussion

There are some children who act out their emotions with tantrums, throwing objects, etc. instead of verbalizing their feelings or using coping skills to regulate emotions. It is important for children to learn to be the "managers" of their emotions. With the support of the therapist this activity reinforces the child to be in control of communicating their feelings and practicing appropriate responses when experiencing various emotions.

Mind Game

Contributed By: Angel Onley-Livingston

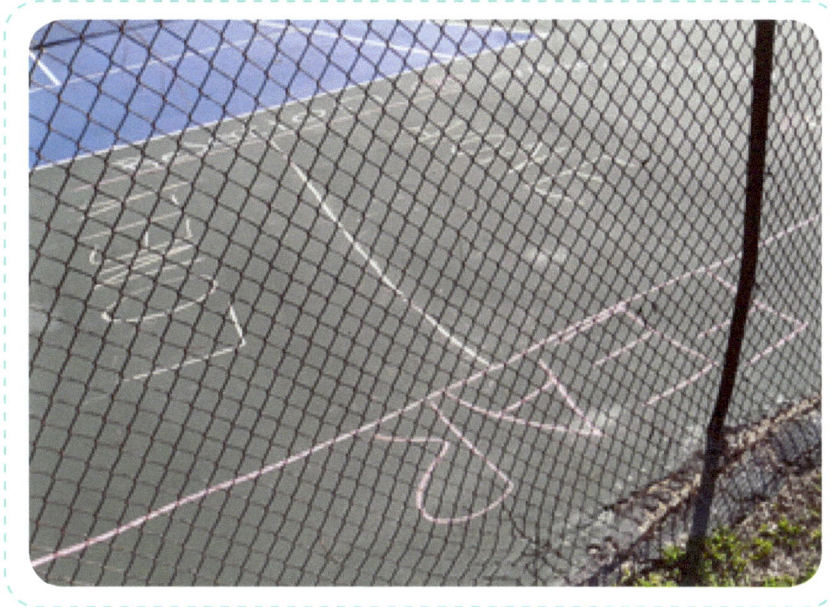

- ○ Treatment Modality: Individual, Group, Family
- ○ Treatment Phase: Engagement, Working

Materials Needed

1. **Big Sidewalk Chalks**
2. **Outdoor Open Space**

Goals of the activity

Demonstrate awareness of fear while understanding of abandonment, feeling lonely, abandoned, and feeling alone. To gain an understanding of emotions and internal conflicts. To explore and identify team building and communication skills.

Activity Steps

Step 1

+ Therapist will use chalk to draw 5 cloud bubbles about 4 ft. in length in a circle on the ground.

Step 2

+ Therapist will direct the client to write a word in each cloud:

Fear, abandonment, feelings, alone, lonely.

Step 3

+ Therapist will direct child to step into the cloud bubble containing the word fear while sharing a time in their life where child's felt fearful. Do so for each cloud bubble until all is complete.

Discussion

During this activity, the therapist can ask the following process questions and discuss with the child. The same steps are followed when working with a family or a small group.

1. What are the differences between feeling lonely and choosing to be alone?

2. Explore emotions of fear and abandonment.

3. Discuss a time where child felt abandoned by a family member or friend.

4. Discuss a time where child felt fearful. Discuss a time where child felt alone.

5. Discuss a time where child felt lonely. How do these times contribute to emotions of anger, sadness, fear, and happiness?

6. How do these feelings and emotions contribute to expectations of family members and friends?

Increasing Your Play Therapy Tool Box

Let Your Feelings Out

Contributed by Sabra Starnes

○ Treatment Modality: Individual

○ Treatment Phase: Engagement or

Materials Needed

1 **Clear jar with lid**

2 **Colored pom poms**

3 **Index cards**

4 **Feelings chart**

Goals of the activity

To help child accurately identify and verbalize feeling.

To increase client's awareness of internal feelings.

To expand the client's feelings vocabulary.

Therapist will label the jar "Feelings Jar" and fill it with different color pom poms. Therapist is recommended to have extra pom poms that do not fit the inside the jar.

Activity Steps

○ **Step 1**

+ Therapist will explain to the child that each colored pom pom represents a feeling of their choice.

○ **Step 2**

+ The child will identify the pom pom colors and separate them.

○ **Step 3**

+ Therapist and child will utilize the index card to write down feelings from a feelings chart. The child will lay out the cards and assign pom poms.

○ **Step 3**

+ The therapist will compare the feelings jar to the child's body and explain how the negative impact of holding in feelings. Showing the jar with one type of feelings can block other types of feelings from entering. This metaphor can be used with the following example:

+ "Think of the jar as your mind and thoughts, you have filled your thoughts with sadness. Since you have not shared your sadness it stays in your mind and it's hard for other feelings to come in. (therapist tries putting a happy pom pom in the jar)"

+ The therapist will facilitate a discussion with the child about methods of releasing feelings. Support systems can also be explored. The therapist will ask open ended questions about the feelings the child selected.

Discussion

This activity works well with younger children or children who present with difficulty expressing their feelings. This activity utilizes a metaphor and provides a visual for easy understanding.

Pom poms come in different sizes and can also be explained that sometimes feelings can be big or small.

Empower Me

Contributed By: Carmen Jimenez-Pride

○ Treatment Modality: Individual, Group, Family
○ Treatment Phase: Engagement, Working, Termination

Materials Needed

1. **Popsicle sticks**
2. **Markers**
3. **Sand tray**
4. **"Power Words" worksheet**
5. **Miniatures**

Goal of the activity

Increasing self-esteem and self-worth in the child by allowing them to connect with their greatness.

○ Step 1

+ Allow the child to pick empowerment words to write on the popsicle sticks.

For younger children or to reuse the sticks, have them cut the words from the "power words" worksheet.

○ Step 2

+ Tape the words to the sticks.

○ Step 3

+ Allow the child to choose several sticks to place in the sand tray. Allow the child to also choose miniatures that best fit the words on the sticks to be placed in the tray.

○ Step 4

+ Lead a discussion on the connection between the miniature and the power word. Encourage the child, group or family to utilize these words daily in their environments, as they continue to focus on self-esteem.

Family Session

Allow the members to create sticks for each other and verbally share and give examples of the connection between the person and the words.

Discussion

There are so many activities that can be done with empowerment words. This is an item that a child can create and take home for ongoing family use and interactions. Having a set of sticks created for the office setting will give a child, group or family a visual of the finished product. The "Power Words" worksheet can be used with the goal of the week activity as a positive self-reflection word to focus on each week.

References:

Van Hollander, Tammi; (2017) Casey's Greatness Wings: Teaching Mindfulness Connection and Courage to Children.

Empower Me Word

Magical	Nice	Forgiving
Hard Worker	Inspiring	Thoughtful
Motivated	Responsible	Thankful
Focused	Funny	Helpful
Generous	Happy	Strong
Great	Calm	Athletic
Mindful	Relaxed	Talented
In Control	Funny	Fun
Helper	Happy	Playful
Honest	Calm	Creative
Smart	Relaxed	Loving
Comforting	Encouraging	Brave
Clever	Good Friend	Kind

Musical Chairs with a Twist

Contributed By: Alisia Mitchell

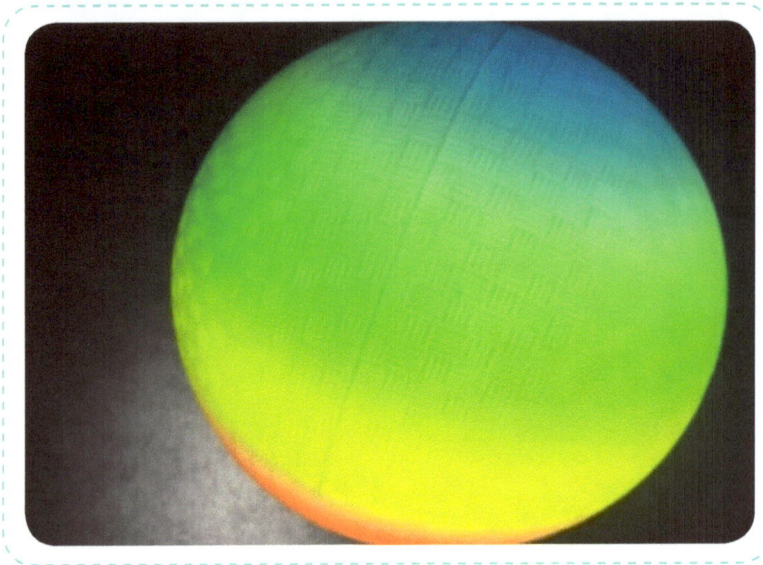

- Treatment Modality: Group or Family
- Treatment Phase: Engagement

Materials Needed

1. One light and bouncy medium to large sized ball
2. Music

Goal of the activity

To practice social skills of sharing, taking turns, and winning/losing a game.

Activity Steps

○ **Step 1**

+ Therapist will direct the child and other participants to make a medium sized circle (about 4 or more feet apart from each other).

○ **Step 2**

+ Therapist will explain the rules of the game, which are similar to the concept of the original "Musical Chairs." Therapist will say, "Has anyone ever played musical chairs? This game is similar, but with a twist. Instead of playing with chairs, we will use this ball. There will be different rules for each round we play. The first rule will be bounce the ball 2 times, then pass it to a different player. You must remember the person you pass the ball to in the circle. There will be music playing in the background, but when the music stops the person holding the ball will be out."

+ **Therapist can have participants create different rules for the participants to take ownership of the game, such as pass it to someone in slow motion, use one hand to pass the ball, pretend to be an animal then pass the ball, etc.

Discussion

According to theorist, Erick Erickson, there are different stages of development children experience. Different ages are associated with various skills learned, such as industry versus inferiority (McLeod, 2018). Children need to learn appropriate social skills to have safe relationships, form bonds with others, practice showing empathy, personal space, being apologetic, patience and other skills needed while interacting with others in different settings. This activity reinforces the importance of such skills to be demonstrated in the home, school, and community environment.

References:

McLeod, S. (2018). Erick Erickson's Stages of Psychosocial Development.

Retrieved from https://www.simplypsychology.org/Erik-Erikson.html

Coping Skills Toolkit

Contributed By: Carmen Jimenez-Pride

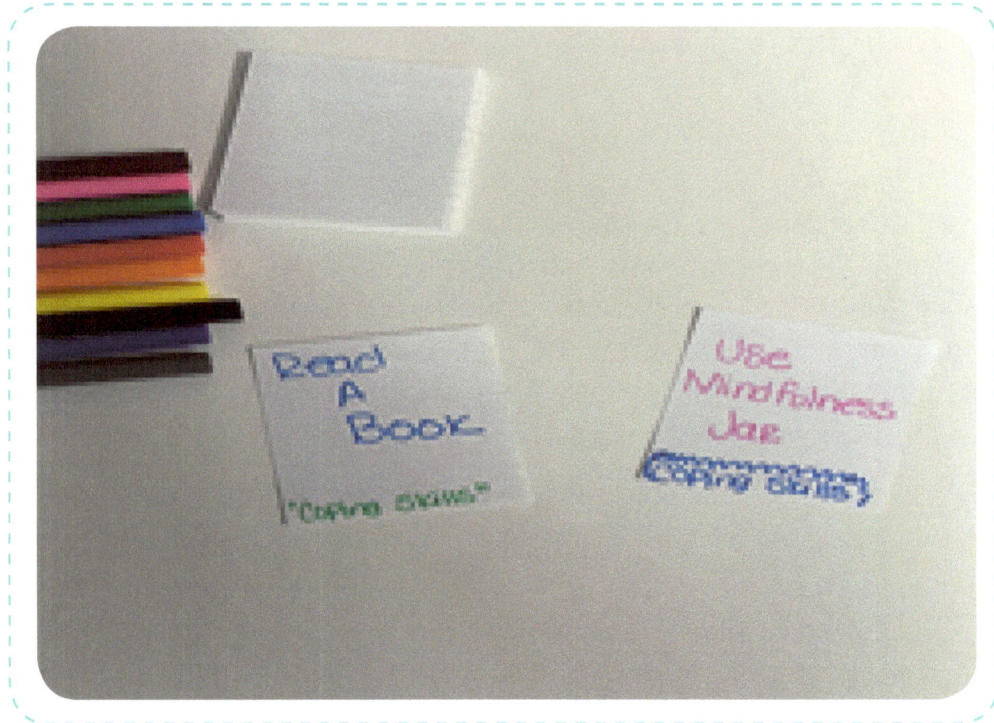

- Treatment Modality: Individual, Group, Family
- Treatment Phase: Engagement, Working

Materials Needed

1. **Markers**
2. **Paper, Card Stock, Index Cards**
3. **Envelope**

Goal of the activity

Creating a list of coping skills to refer to when needed.

Activity Steps

Step 1

Therapist will help the child identify a list of coping skills that can be utilized in various environments/ situations.

Step 2

With the index cards (paper or cardstock to create cards) allow the child to write and draw out the coping skill.

Allow the child to be creative and design an envelope to hold their cards.

Discussion

When children are allowed to engage in the development of a resource there is an opportunity for investment in the use of the resource. It is important for the child to identify activities they want to use as a coping skill. Always be prepared to give some examples by doing the activity yourself during the session.

In the Therapy Room:

The child may need to take a break during the therapy session to reset. Utilizing the coping skill tool kit will help further to increase the use of the resource with the child.

Outside of the Therapy Room:

Therapist is recommended to have a discussion with the parent/caregiver to inquire about situations within the home setting that coping skills can be useful. Encourage the parent/caregiver to prompt the child to utilize their toolkit. The toolkit can be used as an interactive time out or calm down.

My Wheel of Emotions

Contributed By: Alisia Mitchell

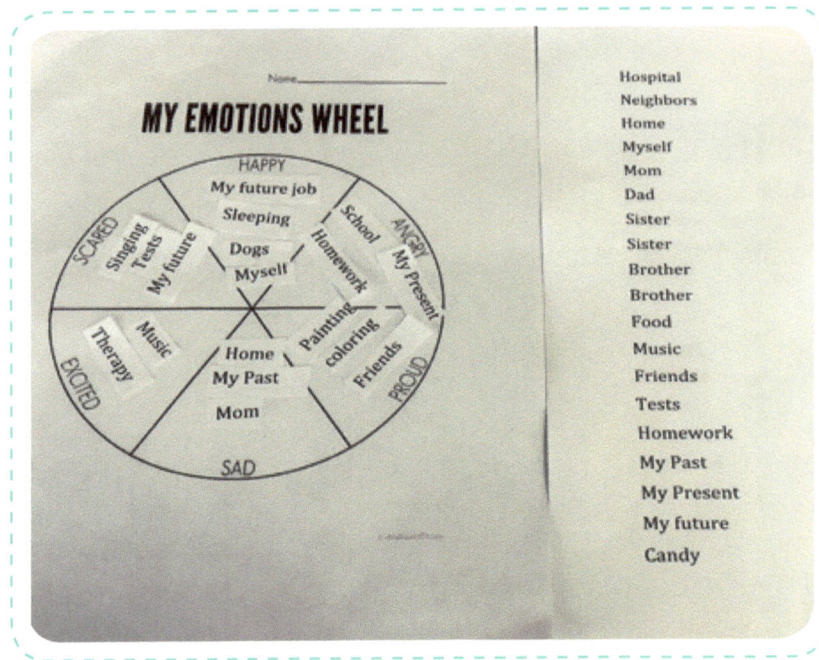

- Treatment Modality: Individual
- Treatment Phase: Engagement

Materials Needed

1. Emotion Wheel (Can be found in the references below)
2. Scissors
3. Glue
4. List of 15+ words related to child's environments and interactions

Goal of the activity

To gain insight of the child's relationships and various settings.

Activity Steps

Therapist will prepare before session begins:

○ Step 1

+ Create a list of different words pertaining to the child's relationships and frequent settings, such as school, stepfather, friends, homework, etc. To support therapist in thinking of different words, please see picture below.

+ **Please note to be mindful to select other words, such as food, toys, painting, reading, holiday's, etc. to have balance in the words chosen. Additionally, therapist can repeat the same word twice on the list in case the child experiences two different feelings about one word. For example, a child may feel happy and sad about school; therefore, the word "school" should be represented twice on the list.

○ Step 2

+ Cut each word out for child to glue on emotion wheel.

To gain insight of the child's relationships and various settings.

○ Step 1

+ Therapist will introduce the activity by explaining, "Here are some emotions we all experience, such as happy, surprised, or worried. Sometimes we feel more than one feeling about things in our life. This will be your emotion wheel. On your wheel, you will paste different words inside each feeling."

**Please note, some children may desire to add a feeling to the emotion wheel. Therapist can allow child to add additional emotions. Also, it is important for therapist to observe any hesitance, or difficulties the child has deciding how they feel about the person/setting, and/or if child prefers to not/avoid selecting a word to put on the emotion wheel.

Discussion

There are many children who do not know how or have difficulty expressing their feelings. It is important to develop a trusting relationship with the child to communicate their feelings.

The role of the therapist is to "hold the space" or sit quietly observing and allowing child the time needed to complete their wheel of emotions. The child may invite therapist into their "space" to help think of where to place the word on the wheel. Therapist can validate child's feelings of being "unsure or hesitant," but allow, child to place the word wherever they desire. This activity provides an avenue for the child to talk about their feelings and associate with their experiences. The therapist will gain awareness on the underlying feelings child may or may not be expressing verbally, but acting out in different situations.

References:

Curly Clues Club. (2018). Exploring Big Emotions with the Emotion Wheel used in the picture below was retrieve from:

https://childhood101.com/wp-content/uploads/2016/03/My-Emotions-Wheel-v2.pdf

Goal of the Week

Contributed By: Carmen Jimenez-Pride

Goals of the Week

Clean Room — Pick up toys, Put up clothes

No talking Back — when directions are given

Use "I feel" Statements

© Teacher Created Resources   TCR 76513 *Smart Start*™ Story Paper

- ○ **Treatment Modality: Individual**
- ○ **Treatment Phase: Engagement, Working**

Materials Needed

1 **Paper**

2 **Crayons, colored pencils, markers**

Goal of the activity

A take home resource for the child and family to outline the goals the child is currently working on. A great resource for family engagement and discussion.

Activity Steps

Step 1

+ Therapist will assist the child to identify a personal goal they would like to work on for the week.

Step 2

+ Once the goal is identified direct the child to design their goal sheet and list their goal.

Discussion

The goal of the week sheet is a resource that is developed in the therapy room and utilized in the home setting. This resource gives the child a visual of what they should focus on during the week. This also provides a resource for the family to discuss goals and progress. Also, can be used as a reminder when behaviors need redirection. For younger children, the following format can be used:

1. Child identified goal

2. Parent identified goal

3. Therapist identified goal

Therapy Room Learning

Based on the identified goals engage the child in role play scenarios to help the child utilize coping skills.

Sculpting Clay Activity

Contributed By: Angel Onley-Livingston

○ **Treatment Modality: Individual, Group, Family**
○ **Treatment Phase: Engagement, Working**

Materials Needed

1. **Sculpting Clay**
2. **Water**
3. **Container (for clay to be molded in)**

Goal of the activity

To process and explore emotions, how the child feels they are viewed by the world. To express difficult emotions such as shame, guilt, remorse, abandonment, rejection, and resentment. To demonstrate coping mechanisms.

Activity Steps

◦ **Step 1**

+ Therapist will introduce the activity to the child and provide clay.

◦ **Step 2**

+ Therapist will direct the child to use clay to mold a representation of how they sees self. Have child use clay to mold a representation of how they think the world sees them.

Discussion

Discuss how we view ourselves the inner and outer self. Discuss how we present ourselves to others. How do we want the world to see us? Remember as the Therapist to remind the child that this is a process of experiencing emotions, not necessarily outward physical appearance.

Values Sticks

Contributed by Sabra Starnes

- ○ **Treatment Modality: Family, Group**
- ○ **Treatment Phase: Engagement**

Materials Needed

1. **Sandtray**
2. **40 Large Popsicle sticks**
3. **List of Values Word Document**

Goal of the activity

Children will be able to identify their core values and how they are connected to them. Children will learn about their values and the values of their family or group members.

Activity Steps

Therapist will prepare prior to the session:

Therapist can prepare a set of value words from the list of values (total of 68 value words in the list) by printing and taping the words to the popsicle sticks. The words can also be written on the sticks with markers.

To begin the session with the child:

Step 1

+ The therapist will lead the child in creating value sticks by cutting out words from the provided list and gluing them to a large popsicle stick. The words can also be written on the sticks using a marker. Store the sticks in a container making the sticks accessibility to the child.

Step 2

+ Therapist will direct the client to select words that most resonate with them. Have the child look for the words that they consider most important and essential to who they are and place them in the sandtray.

+ Therapist will allow the child quiet time to connect with the sand and their words.

Discussion

Brene Brown states, "A value is a way of being or believing that you hold most important." Brené explains that values light your way as you move through life.

She discusses that values can be like in your life can help us to better understand ourselves. Brene Brown explains, "There are no guarantees in the arena. We will struggle. We will even fail. There will be darkness. But if we are clear about the values that guide us in our efforts to show up and be seen, we will always be able to find the light. We will know what it means to live brave. The value sticks activity is a great way to figure out what our values are and how they can help us to better understand ourselves.

References:

Daring Way by Brene Brown

Value Sticks

Accountability Generosity	Loyalty	Caring
Gratitude	Making a difference	Collaboration
Growth	Openness	Commitment
Harmony	Optimism	Community
Health	Patience	Compassion
Home	Peace	Competence
Honesty	Perseverance	Cooperation
Hope	Personal fulfillment	Courage
Humor	Power	Creativity
Inclusion	Pride	Dignity
Independence	Achievement	Diversity
Initiative	Adaptability	Equality
Joy	Adventure	Excellence
Justice	Altruism	Fairness
Kindness	Ambition	Faith
Knowledge	Authenticity	Family
Leadership	Balance	Forgiveness
Learning	Beauty	Freedom
Legacy	Being the best	Friendship
Leisure	Belonging	Fun
Love	Career	

Together We'll Grow

Contributed By: Carmen Jimenez-Pride

- Treatment Modality: Individual, Group, Family
- Treatment Phase: Engagement, Termination

Materials Needed

1. **Small flower pot, jar, plastic cup**
2. **Potting soil**
3. **Grass or flower seeds (quick growing)**
4. **Markers or paint**

Goal of the activity

To teach children about investing, self-care, responsibility and growth.

Activity Steps

○ **Step 1**

+ Decorate the flower pot

○ **Step 2**

+ Plant the seeds in the soil.

Discussion

This activity can be used at any stage of therapy. Depending on the space of your practice location you can keep the flower pots within the office setting. This will allow you to expose the child to responsibility and self-care. The child will be able to care for and visually see the growth of the plant, this can be used as a metaphor to further engage the child with a discussion regarding investment and growth.

To utilize this as a termination activity allow the child to take the plant home and encourage them to keep growing!

Resources: Low cost bulk flower pots can be purchased at oriental trading at a responsible cost. The pot I recommend is the DIY Watch it Grow Seed Pot it can be found at: https://www.orientaltrading.com/diy-watch-it-grow-seed-pots-a2-59_1056.fltr?keyword=Flower+pot

References:

The name of this activity was adopted by the motto of Outspoken Counseling and Consulting LLC "Together We'll Grow".

Communal Sand Tray

Contributed by: Angel Onley-Livingston

- **Treatment Modality: Individual, Group, Family**
- **Treatment Phase: Engagement, Working, Termination**

Materials Needed

1. **Sand Tray**
2. **Sandtray miniatures**

Goal of the activity

To foster communication within a group or family setting. To express visual representation of depression within self. To demonstrate breathing/relaxation technique to decrease anxiety. To explore emotions of anxiety and depression.

Activity Steps

○ Step 1

+ Therapist will direct child to sit down on the floor or at a table. Focus on grounding the child through deep breathing inhaling through the nose for 4 seconds, hold breath for 2 seconds, and breathe out through mouth for 4 seconds.

○ Step 2

+ Direct the child to use the following mindfulness techniques with the phrase below to describe situation that makes them anxious.

I acknowledge I am anxious when_____,

I am depressed when _____,

○ Step 3

+ Therapist will give the directive to choose objects/archetypes from the sand tray figures representing themselves when they are anxious and when they are depressed. Have the clients place archetype in sand tray.

○ Step 4

+ Direct the child share the connection between their figure/archetype and what it means to them.

Discussion

The activity can be completed in individual sessions, family sessions or within a group.

The following questions can be used to deepen the experience:

Discuss how these figures represent who you are.

Discuss how you express and experience anxiety and depression?

Discuss coping skills to reduce and eliminate symptoms of anxiety and depression.

Communal Sandtray: Villain & Hero

Contributed by: Angel Onley-Livingston

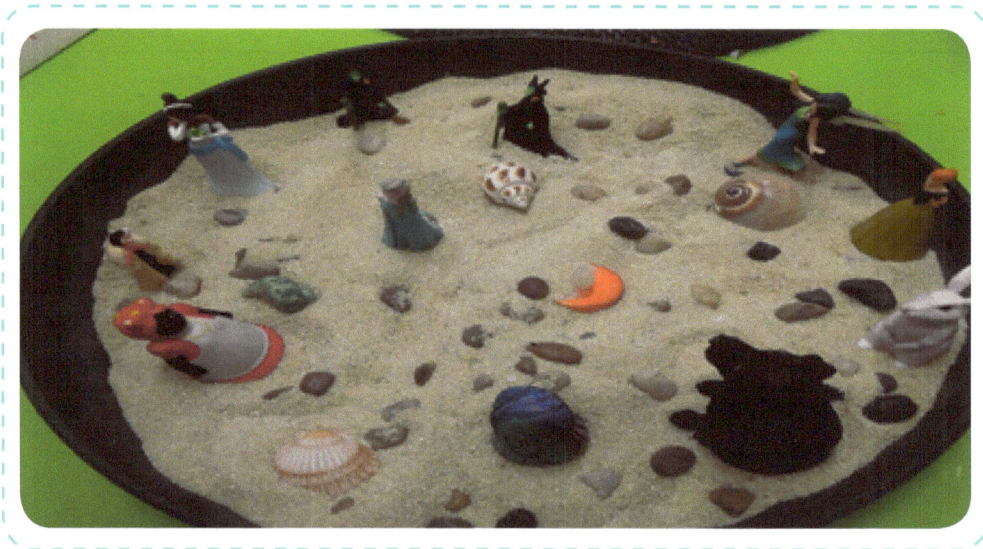

- Treatment Modality: Individual, Group, Family
- Treatment Phase: Engagement, Work, Termination

Materials Needed

1. **Sand Tray**
2. **Sandtray miniatures**

Goal of the activity

To foster communication within group setting. To express anxiety and depression. To demonstrate coping skills. To express the hero and villain parts of their personality.

Activity Steps

○ Step 1

+ Therapist will give the directive to have each individual choose objects/archetypes representing villain side and hero side. Give child 10 minutes for this process.

○ Step 2

+ Therapist will direct child to place both the villain and hero archetypes into sand tray with everyone else's figures.

Discussion

Discuss how family or group members view themselves as a villain. Discuss how they view themselves as a hero. Discuss how the hero side cope with anxiety and depression. Discuss how the villain side cope with anxiety and depression in their behavior. Ask the participants can to be both the villain and the hero and how this shows up in their everyday life experiences? What might need to be changed or worked on if anything.

Rolling Out My Feelings

Contributed By: Alisia Mitchell

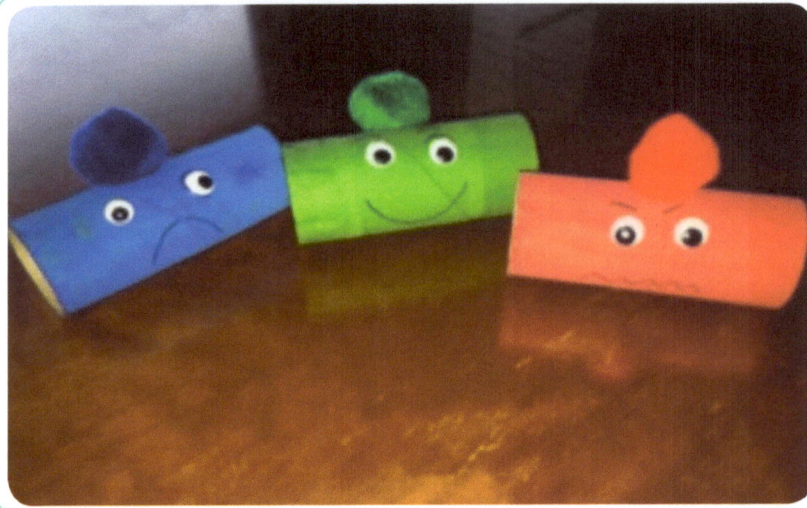

- Treatment Modality: Individual, Family
- Treatment Phase: Engagement

Materials Needed

1. **One empty craft roll (tissue roll or paper towel roll)**
2. **Colored cotton balls**
3. **Glue**
4. **Markers**
5. **Paint and paintbrushes**
6. **Googly eyes**

Goal of the activity

To help identify and regulate child's emotions.

Activity Steps

Session with Client:

○ **Step 1**

+ Therapist and child will sit or stand directly across from each other. Therapist will introduce activity, "Today we are going to learn about feelings. Our feelings are important, but sometimes they are hard to understand. Can you show me a happy face? Can you show me a sad face? Can you show me an angry face?" While therapist is asking each question, therapist will model the facial expression with child.

**Therapist can choose the feelings and allow child a turn to say a feeling and model if desired. This step can be repeated 3 or more times to encourage play, practice, and recognizing facial expressions.

○ **Step 2**

+ Therapist will have paint setup for child to see. Therapist will state, "Now that we have learned happy, sad, and angry (re-state emotions practiced) feelings, let's figure out what colors can help us remember how we are feeling. What color can be happy? What color can sad be? What color can angry be?" Allow child to answer, such as "green" for happy, "blue" for sad, or "red" for angry.

○ **Step 3**

+ Therapist will have the empty craft rolls, paint, and paintbrushes for this step. Therapist will say, "Let's paint the feelings onto each roll." Allow child to paint each empty craft roll with the pre-selected colors assigned to the emotions.

**Please note child may ask you to assist in painting. It is important to encourage the child to paint and "try your best" to reinforce capability, however, therapist can collaborate with child supporting "teamwork." For example, therapist can hold the craft roll while child paints. Also, the entire craft roll does not need to be painted only if desired.

○ **Step 4**

+ After all craft rolls are painted and dried, therapist can direct the child to add googly eyes, cotton balls, and draw face with markers onto craft rolls.

Please note

Child may have difficulties or ask you to draw the facial expressions. Again, it is important to encourage child to "try your best" and draw the face. Therapist can say aloud, "You are working really hard, you are doing good work, you kept going even when it was hard, etc."

Step 1

+ Therapist will prep parent(s) without child in understanding the importance of helping children identify verbally how they are feeling and regulating their emotions, especially after a child has a tantrum or meltdown.

Step 2

+ Therapist, child, and child's parent(s) will sit or stand in a circle. Therapist will introduce activity, "Today we are going to learn about feelings. Our feelings are important, but sometimes they are hard to understand. Let's practice showing a happy face. Next, let's show a sad face. Lastly, show an angry face." Therapist will model the facial expressions with child and parent(s).

Therapist can choose the feelings and allow the child a turn to say a feeling and model if desired. This step can be repeated 3 or more times to encourage play, practice, and recognizing facial expressions.

Step 3

+ Therapist will have paint set aside for this step for child/parent to see. Therapist will state, "Now that we have learned happy, sad, and angry (re-state emotions practiced) feelings, let's figure out what colors can help us remember how we are feeling. What color can be happy? What color can sad be? What color can angry be?" Allow child to answer, such as "green" for happy, "blue" for sad, or "red" for angry.

Step 4

+ Therapist will have the empty rolls, paint, and paintbrushes for this step. Therapist will say, "Let's paint the feelings onto each roll." Allow child and parent to paint each empty roll with the pre-selected colors assigned to the emotions.

**Please note child may ask you or parent(s) to assist in painting. It is important to encourage the child to paint and "try your best" to reinforce capability, however, parent can collaborate with child supporting "teamwork" and attachment with parent/child. For example, parent can hold the roll while child paints. Or, child paints one craft roll while the parent paints the other craft roll. Also, the entire craft roll does not need to be painted only if desired.

Step 5

+ After all craft rolls are painted and dried, therapist can direct child/parent to add googly eyes, cotton balls, and draw face with markers onto rolls.

**Please note child may have difficulties or ask you/parent(s) to draw the facial expressions. Again, it is important to highlight child's capabilities and parent/child joining together to encourage attachment. client's parent can assist child in drawing the facial expressions, however, it is critical parent not "criticize" the child's efforts. Focus should be on "trying your best" and learning to identify/verbalize the feeling not on artwork.

Outside of the therapy room learning. Encouraged the parent to use this new resource in the home setting.

The child and parent can continue to practice what each color means by acting out the emotion at home. When the child is frustrated, the parent can use a craft roll to help child verbalize, "I feel sad," instead of acting out.

Discussion

Parents may have difficulties reading their child emotions, resulting in unwanted behaviors or tantrums. It is important to help young children understand their feelings and learn to calm down in an appropriate manner. This activity supports parents in empowering their child with words, and learning to be in control of their feelings by verbalizing.

Check Me, Check You

Contributed by Sabra Starnes

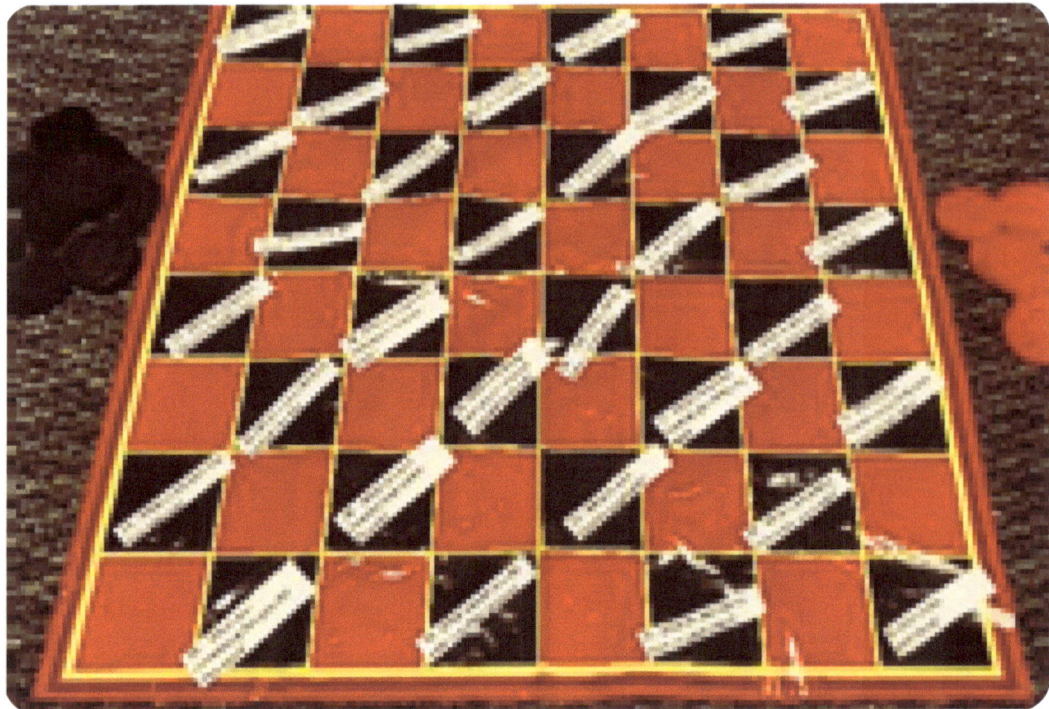

- Treatment Modality: Individual
- Treatment Phase: Engagement

Materials Needed

1. **1 Checkerboard and checkers**
2. **32 questions sheet**

Goal of the activity

To develop rapport between the therapist and child and learn about the child.

Activity Steps

Therapist will prepare prior to session:

Therapist will have the game prepared before use. The 32 questions are taped or glued to the game. The questions are numbered 1-32 and should be placed in order on the board. The pieces are glued or taped so that they are a permanent part of the game board.

○ Step 1

+ Therapist will explain the game board to the child, on each of the black spaces will be question that either the child or the therapist will answer, after they have moved a checker.

○ Step 2

+ The 32 questions involve getting to know you questions that will build rapport between the therapist and child. A question may be asked more than once if landed on a repeatedly. The child can give another answer to the question or can pass if they do not have another answer for that same question.

+ Do not force the child to answer a question allow the child to pass, this will help with building rapport and trust.

Discussion

This is a fun activity to do at the beginning of treatment in developing a positive therapeutic relationship between the child and therapist. If the child has difficulty reading the questions the therapist can read the question for the client.

1. Have you ever been on a plane where did you go?

2. What is your favorite board game?

3. You could be any superhero who would you be why?

4. What is your least favorite subject in school?

5. What do you like to do for fun?

6. What is something that you are really good at?

7. What is something that you are not so good at?

8. Have you ever been on a plane where did you go?

9. What is your favorite board game?

10. What is something that you don't like to do?

11. Who is your favorite teacher?

12. What do you like to play outside?

13. Where do you like to go?

14. What is your favorite dessert?

15. What is your favorite animal?

16. What is your favorite thing to drink?

17. What is something you are thankful for?

18. What was your best Halloween costume ever?

19. What did you do for your last birthday?

20. What is your favorite part of the day?

21. What is something that makes you laugh?

22. What's something that you are proud of yourself for doing?

23. Which household chore do you dislike the most?

24. What is your favorite thing to do with your family? why?

25. What is the best toy that you own?

26. What are your favorite 3 ice cream flavors?

27. What is your favorite vegetable?

28. What is something that makes you laugh?

29. What was something fun you did this week?

Increasing Your Play Therapy Tool Box

30. What would you do with a million dollars?

31. What do you like to have on your pizza?

32. What makes you a good friend?

Marble Jar Friends

Contributed by: Sabra Starnes

- Treatment Modality: Individual or Group
- Treatment Phase: Engagement

Materials Needed

1. Marbles (20-30 Marbles)
2. 2 clear Jars
3. Labels

Goal of the activity

Child will be able to identity and address healthy friendships.

Child will be able to express the characteristic of a good friend.

Child will be able to express and share the characteristics they have, that make them a good friend to others.

Activity Steps

Therapist will prepare prior to the session:

Therapist will create two labeled jars with the following:

How do friends earn my marbles in a relationship?

And how do I earn marbles in a relationship with others?

Therapist will place several marbles in each jar.

○ Step 1

+ Therapist will direct the child to take marbles from the jar and separate them into two piles, next to each of the jars.

○ Step 2

+ Therapist will help the child identify characteristics that they have in themselves or that they want from a good friend.

+ Therapist will ask the client; "How do you earn marbles in a relationship?"

+ For each answer, the client gives put a marble in the jar.

+ The therapist will then have the child select a marble and share a positive characteristic that they want in a friendship.

+ The therapist directs the child to place marbles in the jar for how friends earn their marbles in a relationship.

Example, given to the child:

tells the truth," they put one marble in the jar.

+ If the child has a hard time coming up with characteristics and behaviors of a friend, the therapist will give examples to the client.

This is a great activity to do with a child who has a difficult time making friendships with others, and keeping friends. The child will be able to use each marble to identify the different characteristics that make up a good friend and characteristics that they can talk about that don't make a good friend.

The therapist can discuss friendships and making friends. At the end of this activity the child should be able to have identified both characteristics that they find in themselves that are positive and positive characteristics that they find in others.

The therapist may find it helpful to have a book on building character with children to use a as guide for child to do further work on exploring positive characteristics for themselves and for others.

A good book recommendation therapist can use with clients is What Do You Stand for Kids A Guide to Building Character by Barbara Lewis. It's a book that can help children build positive character traits like caring, cooperation, courage, fairness, honesty, respect, and responsibility.

References:

What Do You Stand For? For Kids: A Guide to Building Character by Barbara Lewis

How do friends earn my marbles in a relationship?

How do I earn marbles in a friendship with others?

Using Your Brain Power

Contributed by: Sabra Starnes

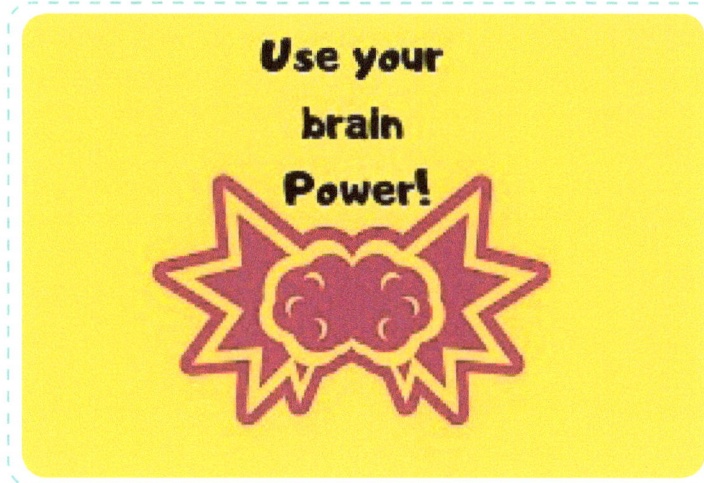

Use your
brain
Power!

- Treatment Modality: Individual or Group
- Treatment Phase: Working

Materials Needed

1. **Book:** Your Fantastic Elastic Brain Stretch It. Shape It by JoAnn Deak (A live reading can be found on YouTube searching the book title. We recommended the Kid Story Time Chanel)

2. **My Brain Power Skills to help Respond and React**

Goal of the activity

Help children understand how their brain works, and how to make good decisions.

Empower children to practice how they can choose to act and respond to challenging situations they face and encourage children to see that they can stretch and grow their thinking and decision-making skills, and problem-solving skills to feel confident and proud.

Activity Steps

Step 1

+ The Therapist will read or play the book to the child or group.

+ Therapist will stop and discuss the different parts of the brain with the child or group.

  The therapist should also ask the child or group members questions about each page and have them share what they think.

Step 2

+ The therapist and child or group members will discuss ways to use brain power. Topics to discuss will include but not limited to asking for help, apologizing or using whole body listening.

Step 3

+ Therapist will ask the child or group members to then identify what brain powers they use.

+ Therapist and child or group members will discuss ways they can use their brain power to help respond to how they are feeling and thinking to help them problem solve when they are struggling, frustrated or stuck on an idea or problem.

Discussion

The "Your Fantastic Elastic Brain Stretch It. Shape it" shares scientific facts on the brain and the different functions of each part.

Written using direct vocabulary and colorful illustrations keeps children interested in the material and encourages children to have a growth mindset by explaining the elasticity your brain has when learning new things, and that making mistakes is the best way to learn.

This psychoeducation activity can help children understand and learn about their brain in a fun and engaging way.

References:

Your Fantastic Elastic Brain Stretch It. Shape It by JoAnn Deak

My Brain Power Skills to help Respond and React

Write or draw

Frontal Cortex is he frontal lobes are involved in motor function, problem solving, spontaneity, memory, language, initiation, judgement, impulse control, and social and sexual behavior.

Amygdala responsible for our emotions, survival instincts, and memory.

Hippocampus with memory, in particular long-term memory.

Help! I'm Feeling Puzzled

Contributed By: Alisia Mitchell

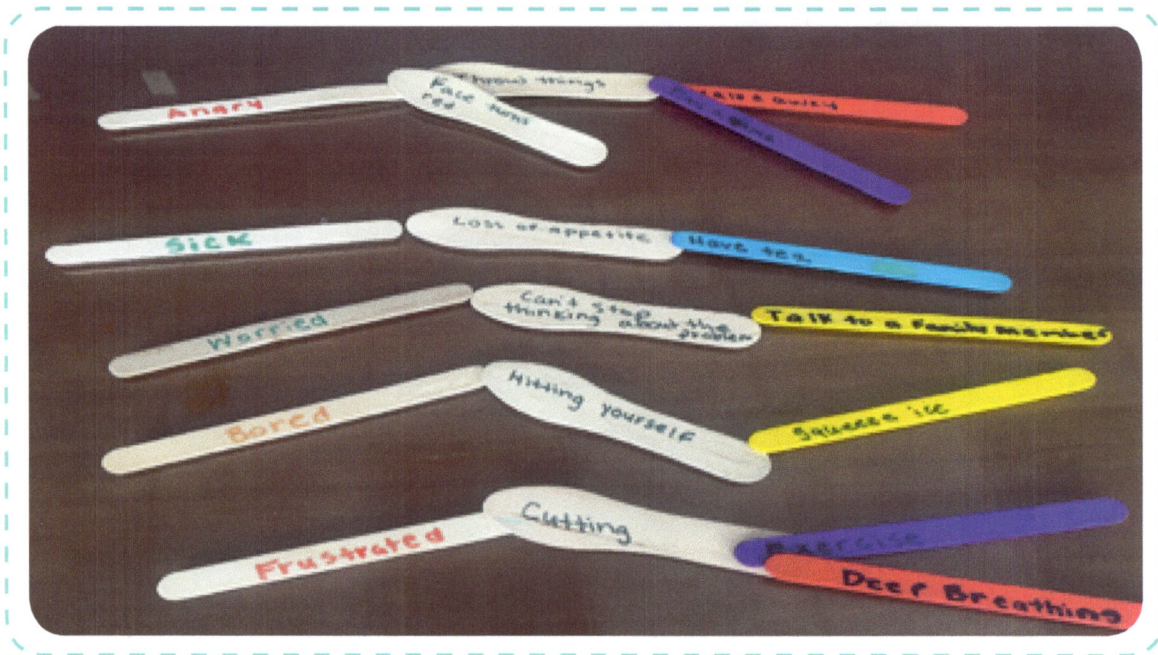

- Treatment Modality: Individual
- Treatment Phase: Engagement

Materials Needed

1. Ten to fifteen plain popsicle sticks
2. Ten to fifteen different shaped, but plain popsicle sticks
3. Fifteen to twenty colored popsicle sticks
4. Permanent marker

Goal of the activity

To help child identify feelings, behaviors, and safe coping skills.

Activity Steps

Therapist will prepare prior to session:

○ **Step 1**

+ Therapist will use a permanent marker to write different feelings on at least 10-15 plain set of popsicle sticks.

○ **Step 2**

+ Therapist will write 10-15 physical behaviors on the second set of plain, but different shaped popsicle sticks. Below is a list of 10 different physical behaviors to support therapist. Please note, it is important to have plain, but different shaped popsicle sticks to decipher between the feeling and behavioral popsicle sticks.

+ **Physical behavior: Hitting, yelling, putting hands over ears, spitting, face turns red, cutting (self-harm), headache, chest hurts, difficulties breathing, shutting down (avoiding or ignoring others/problems).

○ **Step 3**

+ Therapist will write 15-20 appropriate coping skills on colored popsicle sticks. Below is a list of appropriate coping skills to support therapist. In this step, it is critical to have more safe coping skills than the physical behavior popsicle sticks to show there are more alternatives to calm self.

+ **Safe coping skills: Deep breathing, taking a walk, walking away, talking to a trusted adult, coloring/painting/drawing, use play dough, imagining your favorite place, reading a book, sip tea, write in a journal.

Please note, the extra plain, plain/different shaped, and colored popsicle sticks are for child to write their own feelings, behaviors, or copings skills not listed.

Activity steps in session with child:

○ **Step 1**

+ The therapist will facilitate an open discussion to support child in thinking of their feelings and behaviors. Therapist will introduce activity by stating, "We all have emotions, but sometimes we are not sure what to do our feelings. We feel confused or puzzled. For example, sometimes people scream when they are angry. Let's figure out what to do instead with our emotions by making a puzzle."

○ Step 2

+ Therapist will direct client to create a puzzle by taking at least one feeling popsicle stick, and connecting it with at least one behavior child usually exhibits, and lastly choosing a safe coping skill.

Discussion

Many children feel confused and overwhelmed about their feelings, resulting in unsafe behaviors, such as harming their bodies, hitting others, etc. This activity supports the child in recognizing how their feelings are associated or connected with their current behaviors, while practicing safe coping skills learned. Additionally, this activity creates a fun and safe space by providing an opportunity to discuss feelings, current behaviors illustrated, and learning safe coping skills.

Learning About My Feelings

Contributed By: Carmen Jimenez-Pride

- ○ Treatment Modality: Individual, Group, Family
- ○ Treatment Phase: Any

Materials Needed

1. **Focus on Feelings© Learning about my Feelings book**
2. **Paper**
3. **Crayons, Markers, Colored Pencils**
4. **Popsicle sticks**
5. **Glue**

Goal of the activity

Help children learn about their feelings, and how to appropriately express them.

Activity Steps

Therapist will prepare prior to session:

○ Step 1

+ Therapist will utilize the book Focus on Feelings© Learning about my Feelings to help develop the child's understanding of ten core feelings.

○ Step 2

+ With each of the feelings, lead the child in creating their own visual of the feelings. This can be accomplished by drawing a facial expression or identify the feeling with a color.

○ Step 3

+ Therapist will assist the child in gluing the artwork onto a popsicle stick.

Discussion

Focus on Feeling© Learning about my Feelings is written to be used in various settings such as the classroom, therapy room or home setting. This book gives the educator flexibility to teach the feelings utilizing creative methods. This book gives the young reader a sense of independence and achievement of gaining an understanding of the feelings when reading alone.

The feelings sticks can be used in the sand tray to help children process thoughts and feelings.

Family Session

Utilizing the sticks in family sessions will create a safe environment for children to express how they feel regarding what a parent or caregiver is sharing. It is recommended the parent or caregiver is educated on the importance of the use of the sticks and allowing the child to express themselves.

Outside of the therapy room:

Therapist is encouraged to help the parent or caregiver identify situations within the home setting where the sticks can be used. Often times children are asked "why" questions and the parents often do not get an answer. Challenge the parent or caregiver to ask "how did you feel about _____" and encourage the child to use the feeling stick or a feeling word. Giving the child the opportunity to express how they feel can lead to further discussion on the root of the behavior or choice.

References:

Jimenez-Pride, Carmen. (2018). Focus on Feeling© Learning about my Feelings

A Letter to My Parent Who's in Prison

Contributed By: Angel Onley-Livingston

- Treatment Modality: Individual, Group, Family
- Treatment Phase: Working, Termination

Materials Needed

1. **2 Decorative envelopes**
2. **2 Decorative writing papers**
3. **Molding clay (colored)**
4. **Tray for clay figure once it's complete**
5. **Pencils**
6. **Markers**

Goal of the activity

Explore and identify child's emotions, interpersonal resolutions, repressed anger, resentment, abandonment, rejection, disenfranchised grief, grief, and loss around having a parent who is imprisoned.

Activity Steps

Step 1

+ Therapist will verbally discuss with child their feelings of not having their parent with them due to imprisonment. During the discussion therapist will allow the child to create a piece of art with the modeling clay while having this conversation.

Step 2

+ Therapist will discuss with the child what abandonment, rejection, anger, and repressed anger is.

Now connect the child's inability to see their parent on a regular basis due to being imprisoned.

Discuss what the child understands about prison or where their parent is.

Therapist will direct the child to write a letter (to themselves, a character/superhero or piece of art they created) about how they now feel about their parent and prison.

Step 3

+ Therapist will allow the child to choose to work with the same piece of art created from the modeling clay or to create another figure. This time follow the same steps but inform child that they will be doing the same activity, but the outcome will be writing the letter to their parent in prison.

*Obtain the child's permission or permission of legal guardian for the letter to be mailed to the parent.

(This activity will take two sessions to complete. Do not feel the need to rush the child through the activity. The modeling clay will remain moist for at least a year.)

Discussion

Therapist can process with the child the following questions:

1. What they know about what led the parent going to prison?

2. Were they there when the parent was arrested?

3. What did they see, hear, smell, taste, feel, touch?

4. What are the sounds or images they remember from that time?

5. How does that make them feel?

What I Wish For You

Contributed By: Sabra Starnes

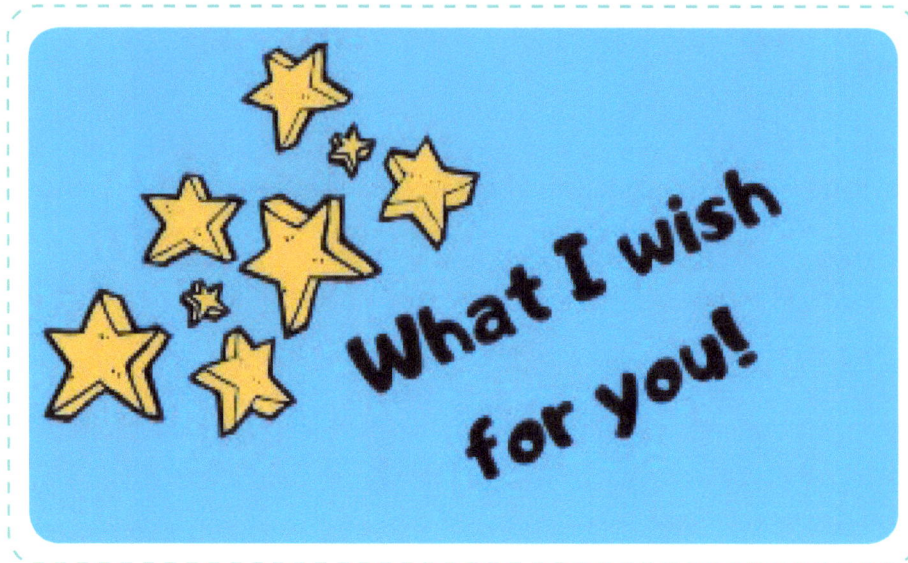

- **Treatment Modality: Family**
- **Treatment Phase: Working**

Materials Needed

1. **Book:** I Wish You More by Amy Krouse Rosenthal and Tom Lichened.
2. **Markers or Crayons**
3. **Blank paper**

Goal of the activity

To identify positive things that family members, hope for each other.

To create visual cues with positive statements for each family member to share and remember.

To increase communication and listening between family members.

Activity Steps

Therapist will prepare prior to the session:

Therapist will cut out 4 to 6 stars for each family member attending the session.

To begin with the family:

○ **Step 1**

+ Therapist or caregiver will read the book, as each page is read the family is allowed time to share wishes for each other that relate to wish on the page.

○ **Step 2**

+ Therapist will pass out 4 to 6 stars to each family member along with markers or crayons.

○ **Step 3**

+ Therapist will prompt each family member to complete the sentence "I wish on this star for you". Explain to the family to share what they wish for members of their family. Depending on the number of family members present average two to three stars per family member.

○ **Step 4**

+ Therapist will engage the family members in a discussion about their stars. Therapist will engage each family member to share a behavior they feel they should change or start to meet the goal on the star.

Discussion

This activity uses a bibliotherapy resource to help engage in the presented activity. The family is able to further the discussion about the wishes they have for each other and utilize creative arts methods to create a visual of their wishes. The hands on creative arts activity further helps the family invest in the session and gives them an opportunity for further learning within the home environment.

The family should be encouraged to use their stars to redirect behaviors, and create a calm and relaxing effect. This activity also encourages family time outside of the therapy room.

I Am a Gift, You Are a Gift

Contributed By: Alisia Mitchell

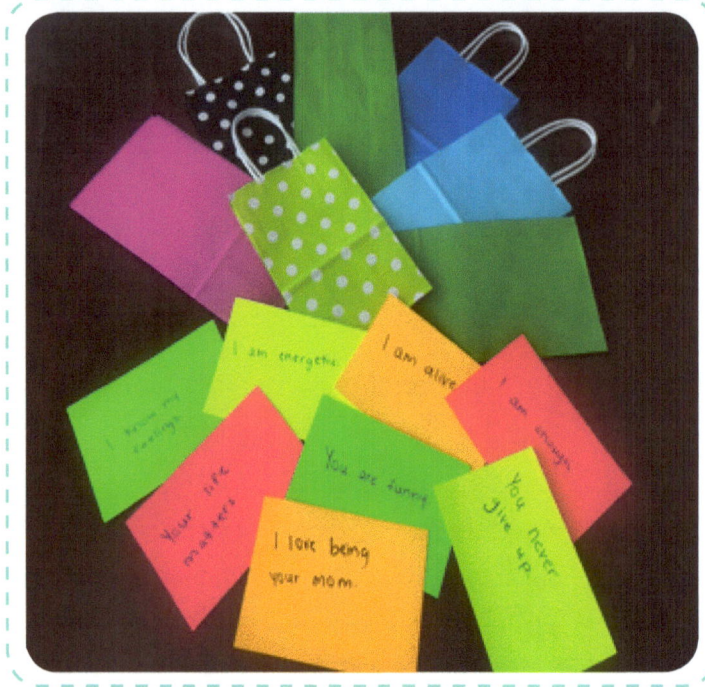

- ○ **Treatment Modality: Individual, Family, Group**
- ○ **Treatment Phase: Working**

Materials Needed

1. **Gifts bags for each participant**
2. **15+ Note cards**
3. **Candy or small snack (optional)**

Goal of the activity

To identify positive strengths and increase self-esteem about child and/or others present.

Activity Steps

Therapist will prepare prior to session:

Therapist will create at least 15+ note cards with positive characteristics written on each card. Positive characteristics can be "I am funny, I have curly hair, I am creative, etc."

To begin session with an individual client:

○ **Step 1**

+ Therapist will provide the individual with a gift bag of his or her choice.

○ **Step 2**

+ Therapist will place all cards written in front of the client. Therapist will begin, "Everyone was born with a gift. Gifts of learning, being helpful, artistic, and more. Today, we will learn about your gifts. You will select different cards you believe are gifts about yourself and place into your bag. We will read at the end."

  **Please note the client may have trouble selecting their "gifts." It is important to help client reflect on past/current personal achievements or highlight strengths (singing, being patient, cooking, sharing, etc.) to support clients in thinking of their "gifts."

○ **Step 3**

+ After client has selected their "gifts," therapist can facilitate a discussion in reviewing the client's strengths/positive characteristics.

Group or family session:

Therapist will prepare before session: Therapist will prepare two different sets of cards for individual and group/family positive characteristics cards. There should be a variety of "I" and/or "You" statements referring to the individual or participants. For example, "I am funny, I have curly hair," "You are loving, You know how to fix things."

The number of cards will depend on the number of participants in the session.

A good "rule of thumb" is to have at least 3 individual and 3 group/family positive characteristics cards for each participant. For example, if you have 5 people in the group there will be 3 individual and 3 group/family positive characteristics cards for each person. In total, there will be 30 cards completed (15 individual and 15 group/family cards). Additionally, there will need to be multiples of the same statement, such as "I am hopeful, I am hopeful," written more than once in order for all participants to have the opportunity to select the expression.

○ **Step 1**

+ Therapist will provide the individual with a gift bag of his or her choice.

○ **Step 2**

+ Then therapist will place all cards written in front of group/family. Therapist will say, "Everyone was born with a gift. Gifts of learning, being helpful, artistic, and more. Today, we will learn about our gifts. First, you will select different cards you believe are gifts about yourself and place into your bag. After selecting gifts about yourself, choose cards that you believe are gifts about the people around you and place in their bags. After finishing each person will read their own gifts they selected and what others have said about them."

○ **Step 3**

+ After group/family has selected their "gifts," therapist can facilitate a discussion in reviewing their strengths/positive characteristics.

Discussion

According to Alfred Adlerian, there are 4 mistaken goals children exhibit, "undue attention, power, revenge, and assumed inadequacy" (Adlerian, 2018). This intervention focuses on assumed inadequacy or "I won't do things right so I will not try" (Adlerian, 2018). This activity reinforces the child's need to feel capable, proud, and learning to accept themselves and others.

References:

Alfred Adler Institute of Northwestern Washington. (2018). Adlerian Child Guidance Principles. Retrieved from http://www.adlerian.us/guid.htm

Dear John, Dear Jane

Contributed By: Carmen Jimenez-Pride

- Treatment Modality: Individual, Family, Group
- Treatment Phase: Engagement, Working, Termination

Materials Needed

1. **Notebook, paper**
2. **Pencil**
3. **Crayons, markers**

Goal of the activity

To help children with problem solving.

Activity Steps

○ **Step 1**

+ Ask the child to pretend they are writers for a newspaper column called Dear John or Dear Jane. Explain to them that a reader of the paper has written to them for help solving a problem similar to something they are struggling with. (Such as being bullied, getting angry, fear, etc.)

○ **Step 2**

+ Help the child to write a letter to the reader giving them some advice about how to solve the problem. Guide them in identifying things they have learned or tried that may help the reader.

Discussion

This activity can be used throughout treatment to assist the child with identifying various tools they have learned during the course of treatment. This will help promote problem solving skills and allow the child to use inner strength to target problems and reach goals. This activity can be used as evaluation to assess the skills the child has developed.

Making a copy of the letter and allowing the child to take it home will be a good reminder when needed. The letters can be put together and given to the child as their own self-help reference book.

Teamwork Makes the Dream Work

Contributed By: Angel Onley-Livingston

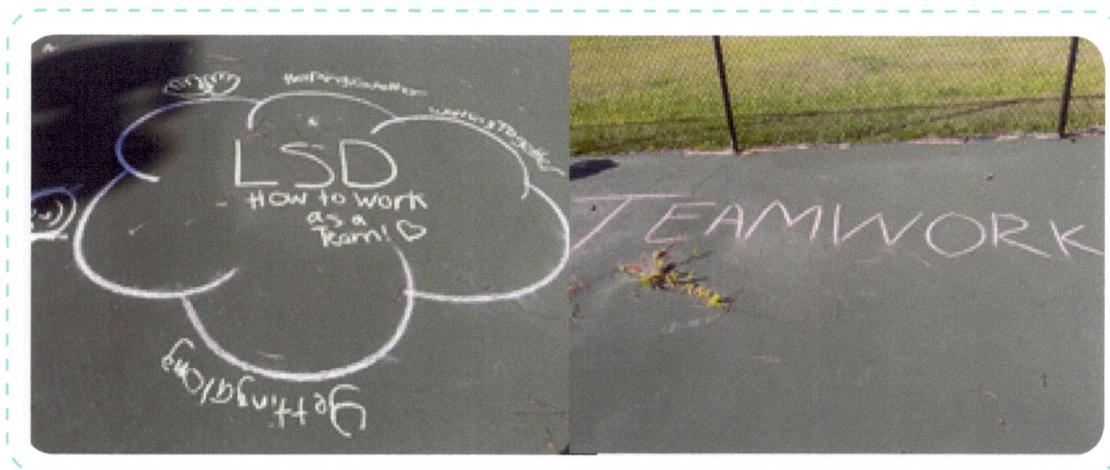

- Treatment Modality: Individual, Group, Family, Team Building
- Treatment Phase: Engagement, Working, Termination

Materials Needed

1. **Big Sidewalk Chalk**
2. **Outdoor Space or chalkboard**

Goal of the activity

Explore the importance of being able to work with others. To gain understanding and awareness of working together in school, sports, or within families. To identify child's strengths and weaknesses that prevents them from being productive and efficient in a group setting. To gain an awareness of internal conflicts and inner emotions of trust around fear of rejection, abandonment, and getting hurt. (You can replace the word teamwork, with the word family, basketball, football, soccer team, or chess team.)

Step 1

+ Draw out 3 cloud bubbles 4-5 ft. in length in a straight line.

Step 2

+ Use chalk to write out words above cloud 1. fear 2. anger 3. stress.

Step 3

+ Have child use chalk to take turns writing who or what makes them feel that way in each respected cloud bubble.

Discussion

Discuss what are the limitations that prevent you from joining a group or extracurricular activity? Discuss internal conflicts while on a family outing or trying to spend time with family. Identify and discuss struggles with gaining and giving trust out of fear of rejection, abandonment, and getting hurt.

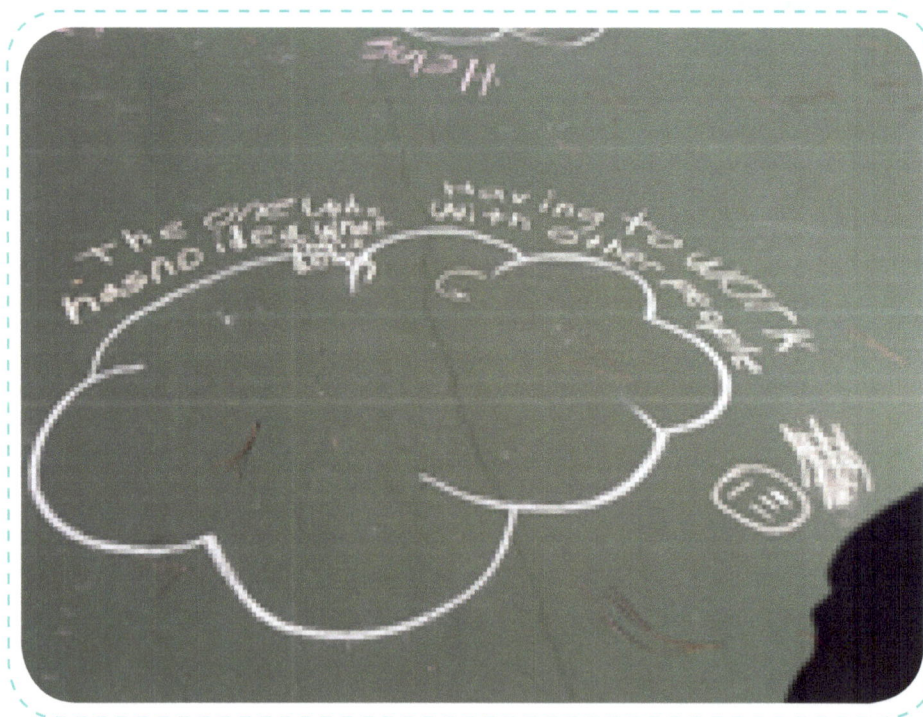

Hopes, Wishes and Dreams

Contributed By: Sabra Starnes

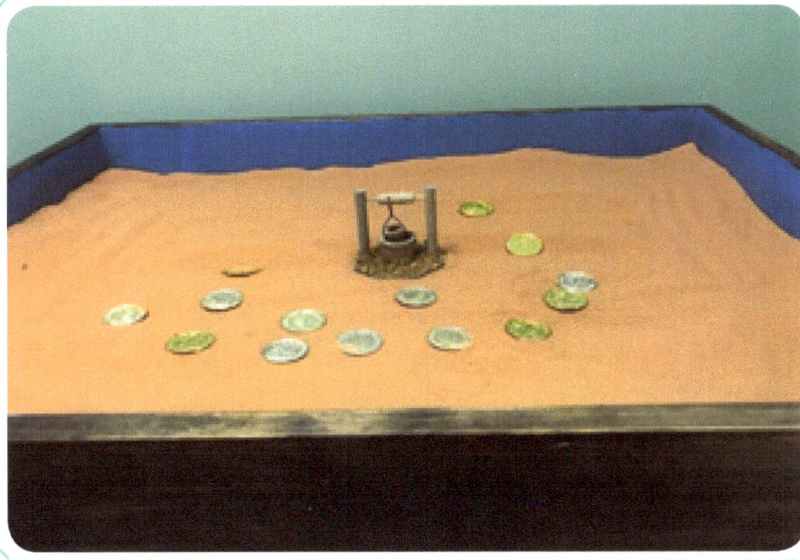

- **Treatment Modality: Individual**
- **Treatment Phase: Engagement, Working, Termination**

Materials Needed

1. **Sand tray**
2. **Wishing well miniature & play coins**
3. **Paper**

Goals of the activity

To increase client's sense of competence.

To help the client engage in short and long goal setting.

To help the client to identify and address the hopes, wishes and dreams they have for themselves.

o **Step 1**

+ Therapist will utilize directive sandtray methods by giving the child coins to put into the sand and explaining the coins represent their hopes, dreams and wishes for themselves.

o **Step 2**

+ Allow the child time in the sand with the coins. Offer the child paper to write down what the coins means to them. (The child has the option to share as they place each of the coins in the sand tray or wait until the end.)

Discussion

The hopes, wishes and dreams sand tray activity is a directive sand tray activity to encourage the child explore verbally and non-verbally things that they either wish, hope or dream for themselves now or in the future.

After the child has completed their tray the therapist takes a picture and keeps it.

It can be used for future discussion in other sessions giving the child opportunity to further explore and discuss the sandtray.

My Safety Circle

Contributed By: Alisia Mitchell

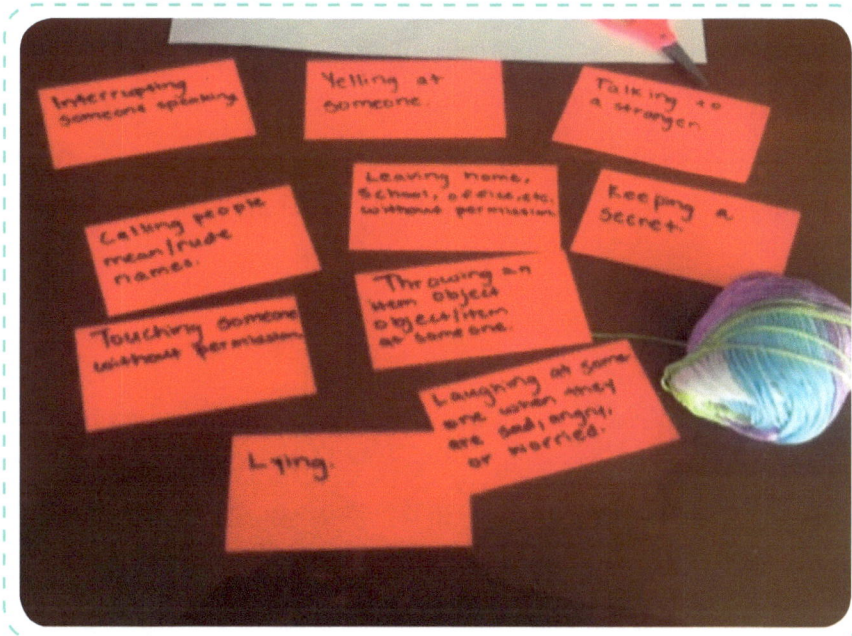

- Treatment Modality:Family, Group
- Treatment Phase: Working

Materials Needed

1. **Poster board**
2. **Markers**
3. **Colorful yarn**
4. **Scissors**
5. **5-10 Note cards**

Goal of the activity

To address appropriate and inappropriate emotional and physical boundaries.

Therapist will prepare before session begins:

Therapist will create [at least] five different note cards with inappropriate emotional and physical boundaries. Please see a list of examples below:

Inappropriate emotional boundaries: Interrupting someone when speaking, yelling at someone, lying, gossiping, calling someone names, blaming, etc.

Inappropriate physical boundaries: Touching someone without permission, hitting someone, throwing objects, taking someone's items without permission, reaching into someone's food, running into someone's room/office without knocking, etc.

To begin session:

Step 1

+ Therapist will direct the family/group to form a circle standing 2-4 feet apart from each other. Then therapist will make one medium to large size circle with the yarn wide enough for all participants to hold together. Therapist will be standing on the outside of the circle observing family/group.

Step 2

+ Therapist will begin, "The circle you are holding is a safety circle. The safety circle represents trust. What would happen to the safety circle if [therapist will select and read different note cards one at a time] someone interrupted a person while speaking?" Allow participants to answer. Therapist may probe family/group to assist, such as "How would the person feel?" After one card has been read, the therapist will use the scissors to cut one part of the circle. This process (Step 2) will be repeated until all note cards are read and the original circle is in pieces.

Step 3

+ Therapist will ask participants, "What happened to our safety circle and how does it feel?" Participants may answer, "Broken, it's all over the place, sad, etc." Next therapist will say, "Let's work on putting our safety circle back together."

Step 4

+ For each previous card read, allow participants to think of a different solution to represent an appropriate boundary. For example, "interrupting someone" is now "waiting your turn before you speak." The participants will tie a knot for each appropriate boundary resulting in a new circle.

○ **Step 5**

+ After the circle is formed, participants will sit together to create "Safety Rules" on the poster board for their family/group (waiting patiently, apologize, ask permission to give someone a hug, etc.)

Discussion

Boundary setting is a critical part of child development supporting appropriate interactions with others in the home, school, and community. Often times poor boundary setting results in mistrust, brokenness, or betrayal. As the therapist, it is important to highlight/stay in the metaphor with participants of how emotional/physical boundaries lead to brokenness between friends, classmates, adults, or family members. However, learning about appropriate boundaries can support/heal past wounds. This activity will aid in increasing awareness of inappropriate boundaries and establishing new ways for families to practice their safety rules.

Feelings Comic Strips

Contributed By: Angel Onley-Livingston

- Treatment Modality: Individual, Group, Family
- Treatment Phase: Engagement, Working, Termination

Materials Needed

1. Blank piece of drawing paper Large to make Comic Strip
2. Crayons
3. Markers
4. Colored Pencils

Goal of the activity

To explore emotions of anger, sadness, anxiety, fear, and happiness. To explore coping skills regarding behavior towards internal and external conflicts. Identify and demonstrate behavior around conflicts. To explore inner and external conflicts.

Activity Steps

○ **Step 1**

+ Therapist will direct child to fold the large piece of paper into 4 or 6 equal columns (either will work). Then fold the paper in half using longer side of paper to meet other longer side of paper.

○ **Step 2**

+ Therapist will direct the child to trace lines with one or several colors to give boundaries to reflect comic strip squares.

○ **Step 3**

+ Therapist will direct the child draw characters representing their villain side and hero side as their characters cope with anger, anxiety, and depression. Direct child writes conversations in comic strip bubbles in regard to their anger, anxiety, and depression. Direct child draws out scenes in each comic bubble around how they cope with anger, anxiety, and depression.

Discussion

Discuss and explain anger, anxiety, and depression. How does your villain side cope with anger, anxiety, and depression? How does your hero side cope with anger, anxiety, and depression? How are our inner conflicts portrayed through our villain side and hero side? Discuss coping skills child can incorporate to reduce and/or eliminate anger, anxiety, and depression.

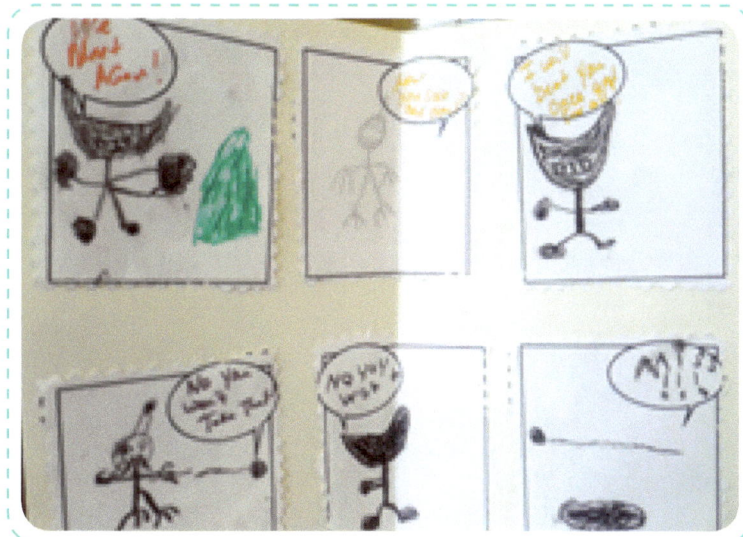

Activity Steps

○ **Step 1**

  + Therapist will assist the child to identify a personal goal they would like to work on for the week.

○ **Step 2**

  + Once the goal is identified direct the child to design their goal sheet and list their goal.

Discussion

The goal of the week sheet is a resource that is developed in the therapy room and utilized in the home setting. This resource gives the child a visual of what they should focus on during the week. This also provides a resource for the family to discuss goals and progress. Also, can be used as a reminder when behaviors need redirection. For younger children, the following format can be used:

1. Child identified goal

2. Parent identified goal

3. Therapist identified goal

Therapy Room Learning

Based on the identified goals engage the child in role play scenarios to help the child utilize coping skills.

Share How Great You Are

Contributed by Sabra Starnes

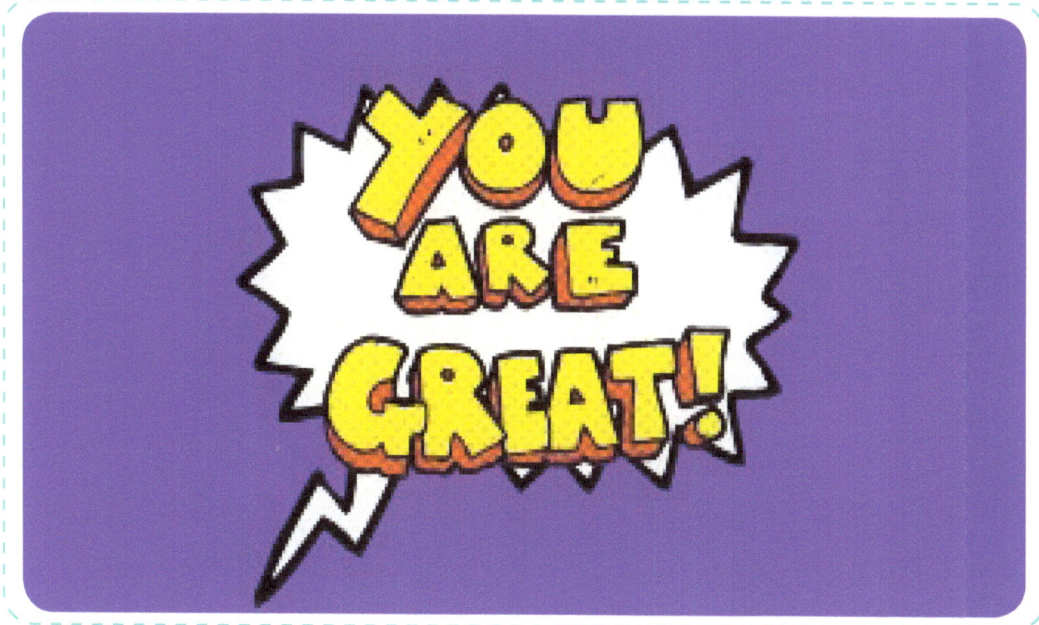

YOU ARE GREAT!

○ **Treatment Modality:** Individual and Group
○ **Treatment Phase:** Engagement, Working

Materials Needed

1 **8 Large Popsicle Sticks**

2 **Glue**

3 **Scissors**

4 **Book:** To Your Greatness by Catherine Stafford and Howard Glasser

Goal of the activity

To increase child self-concept and increase self-worth.

Therapist will prepare prior to session

Therapist will print and cut coordinating worksheet or create 5 colored cards based on the following:

Blue- Something you are grateful for

Green – Something you are proud of yourself for

Red- Something you wish for.

Purple- Something you hope for.

Yellow- Something you dream about.

To begin the session with the child:

○ **Step 1**

+ Therapist will read the book "To Your Greatness", make attempts to have the child read as well. Lead the child in a discussion about the book.

○ **Step 2**

+ Therapist or client will read the 5 greatness sentences and complete each statement by writing the response on the card.

○ **Step 3**

+ Glue card on each of the popsicle sticks.

○ **Step 4**

+ Therapist will lead the child in a discussion regarding the responses. The therapist will encourage positive thinking and self-talk.

References:

To Your Greatness by Catherine Stafford and Howard Glasser

Something you are grateful for..

Something your proud of yourself for…

Something you Wish For…

Something you Dream About…

Something you want to change about how yourself…

Pathway to my Feelings

Contributed By: Alisia Mitchell

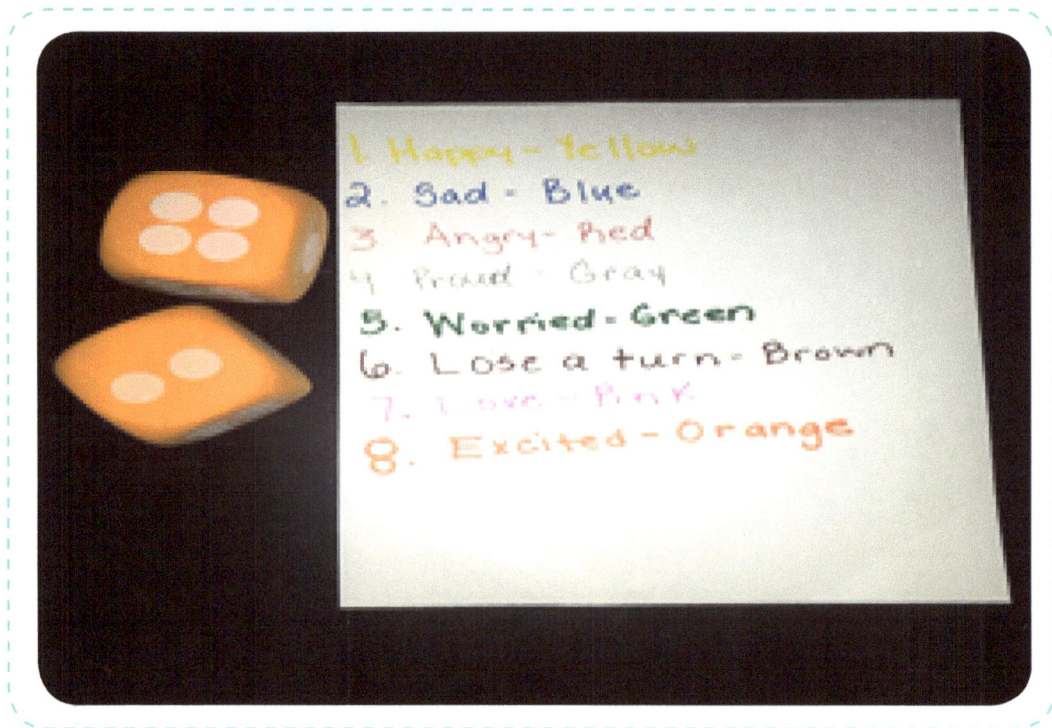

- **Treatment Modality:** Family, Group
- **Treatment Phase:** Working

Materials Needed

1. **Set of dice**
2. **13-15 different colored craft felt**
3. **Paper and Markers**

Goal of the activity

To practice social skills of patience, taking turns, listening, winning/losing and expressing feelings verbally

Activity Steps

Therapist will prepare prior to session

Therapist will print and cut coordinating worksheet or create 5 colored cards based on the following:

Blue- Something you are grateful for.

Green – Something you are proud of yourself for.

Red- Something you wish for.

Purple- Something you hope for.

Yellow- Something you dream about.

To begin the session with the child:

○ Step 1

+ Therapist will begin by aligning craft felt in a vertical line for the game path. An example is written below. Each felt represents a time participant experienced the emotion, such as "I felt sad when…" or "I feel proud when…"

  **It is recommended to begin and end with an emotion the child feels safe in expressing, such as "happy or silly" then other challenging emotions. Please see example below to align felt/emotion:

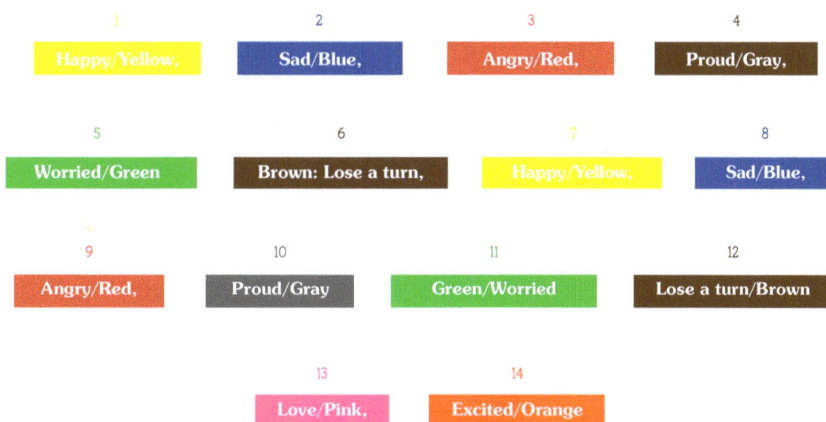

1	2	3	4
Happy/Yellow,	Sad/Blue,	Angry/Red,	Proud/Gray,

5	6	7	8
Worried/Green	Brown: Lose a turn,	Happy/Yellow,	Sad/Blue,

9	10	11	12
Angry/Red,	Proud/Gray	Green/Worried	Lose a turn/Brown

13	14
Love/Pink,	Excited/Orange

**Please note the brown colored felt is intentionally placed, as number 6 and 12 for purposes of the highest number on the dice is 6, which supports child practicing social skills of winning/losing. However, child can play as many times to do their best to get to the end of the pathway.

Other suggestions for brown: Lose a turn, start from the beginning of game path, swap with another player, move two space backwards, etc. (Participants can make up rule).

Step 2

Write each emotion with marker on paper to support child in distinguishing what each felt represents.

> To begin session:

Step 1

+ Therapist will state: "We are going to play a game to help us talk about our feelings. Each person will start at the beginning of the game path. The person who starts will roll their dice on the floor to see what number it lands in order to move up the game path. Each color will represent a time you felt the emotion, such as "I felt happy when..." or "I feel sad when..." Then the next person will roll their dice to take their turn. In order to get to the end of the game path you must roll the exact number on the dice to get to the end."

+ **Therapist will give an example, if you are at happy [second to the last emotion], you must roll a "1" to get to the last feeling, which is silly. If you a roll a "2" or more with the dice, you remain at happy. The game will continue with each person taking turns to get to the end of the game path.

Discussion

This intervention motivates children to express their feelings safely while having fun. Playing activities/games to assist children in learning about patience, taking turns, listening, winning/losing etc. assists in managing impulse control. Therapist can encourage child to continue playing until getting to the end of the game path. For example, if child loses the first round, therapist can play another round with the child or remind child there will be other opportunities to play again. Additionally, therapist can support the child in saying, "You did your best, you worked really hard to get to the end of the game path, you were able to remember different times you felt each emotion, etc."

Feelings Scale

Contributed By: Carmen Jimenez-Pride

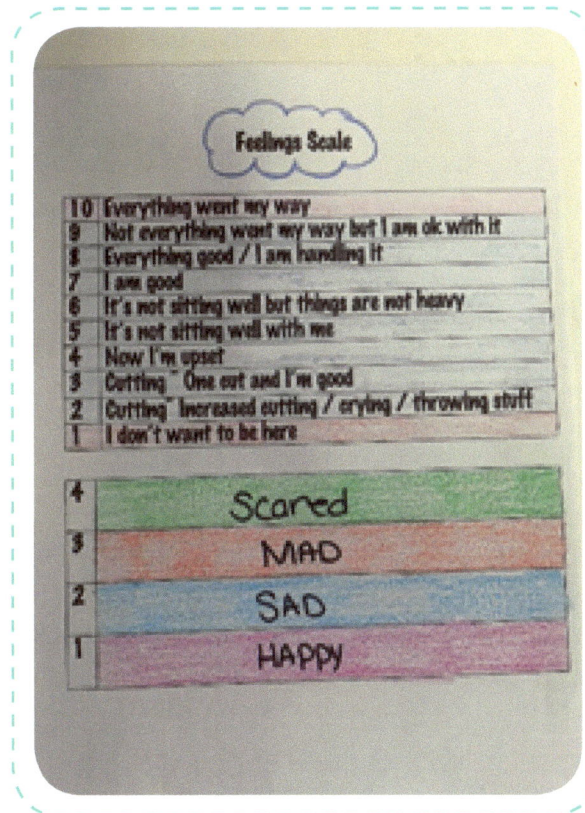

Feelings Scale

10	Everything went my way
9	Not everything went my way but I am ok with it
8	Everything good / I am handling it
7	I am good
6	It's not sitting well but things are not heavy
5	It's not sitting well with me
4	Now I'm upset
3	Cutting~ One cut and I'm good
2	Cutting~ Increased cutting / crying / throwing stuff
1	I don't want to be here

4	Scared
3	MAD
2	SAD
1	HAPPY

- ○ Treatment Modality: Individual, Family
- ○ Treatment Phase: Engagement, Working

Materials Needed

1. Feelings scale worksheet
2. Markers, Crayons

Goal of the activity

Help children verbally express various feelings in a scale form.

Activity Steps

Younger Children

Cut the scale worksheet in half or to the number you want the child to focus on. Identify several feelings often expressed by the child. Write them in the block. Have the child pick a color and assign to the feeling.

Older Children

Utilizing the Feelings scale worksheet lead the child with identifying a statement that best describes their lowest thought and write that on number one. Lead the child with identifying a statement that describes their best day and write that on number ten.

Discussion

Assure that you make a copy of the scale to use when needed in session. This scale can be used in journaling, prompts for homework, or expressing feelings when facing difficult situations. The feeling scale can be used as a daily check-in during therapy sessions. When working with families, this scale can be used to promote communication within the home. Have the child review the scale with their parents, if the child feels comfortable share a copy with the parents. Direct the parent to allow the child to give a number within the home setting at the onset of a conflict. This will still promote communication and allow the child to gather their thoughts and feelings prior to further discussing the situation.

Superhero Video Activity

Contributed By: Angel Onley-Livingston

- Treatment Modality: Individual, Group, Family
- Treatment Phase: Engagement, Working, Termination

Materials Needed

1. **Video Camera/Mobile Phone/Tripod**
2. **Example of completed Comic Strip**
3. **Paper pre-cut Masks**
4. **Pre-cut Packaged Body Figures Boys and Girls**
5. **Plain Paper**
6. **Markers, Crayons, Colored Pencils**
7. **Sandtray figures**
8. **Basket to collect Sandtray figures**

Goal of the activity

To understand emotional and interpersonal conflicts. To build self-esteem while using coping skills to overcome inner conflicts and intrusive thoughts. To exemplify acquired skills in overcoming adversity within self, family, and team.

○ **Step 1**

+ Therapist will direct child create and design pre-cut mask using art supplies. Therapist will direct the child to design pre-cut package body figures.

○ **Step 2**

+ Therapist will direct child choose archetypes from sand tray as needed for comic strip scene.

○ **Step 3**

+ Therapist should now set up camera/video camera in a room or space for video recording (assure written consent is on file for recording). Have child put on mask to conceal and protect their identity.

○ **Step 4**

+ Client will read and act out their comic strip along with props or objects they have created from paper or sand play figure/archetypes. Use props to act out and role-play in coping with emotions through comic strip.

Discussion

Therapist is recommended to discuss coping with internal and emotional conflicts. Discuss and explain to child that sometimes we are happy and then sad, and sometimes like superheroes we are courageous and bold or like the villain, we can be mean and spiteful. Discuss opposites that continue to conflict on the inside or our inner self. Discuss how we express our emotions through behavior.

Ask the following questions:

Do you view yourself as the villain or the hero?

Can you be both?

Affirmations in the Sand

Contributed By: Sabra Starnes

- Treatment Modality: Individual, Group, Family
- Treatment Phase: Working

Materials Needed

1. Sandtray and miniatures
2. Marker
3. Construction paper or index card
4. Manifest Your Magnificence Affirmation Cards (optional)

Goal of the activity

This is a directive sandtray activity for children to create a visual and written affirmation about themselves. Child will develop or increase positive affirmations to inspire them to be able to identify and make positive statements about themselves. Also, to improve client's interpersonal skills.

Cut the scale worksheet in half or to the number you want the child to focus on. Identify several feelings often expressed by the child. Write them in the block. Have the child pick a color and assign to the feeling.

Activity Steps

○ Step 1

+ Therapist goes over affirmation cards with the child. Therapist will ask the child to choose four affirmation cards they can relate to. If the child is having trouble give the time to review the cards to connect what best fits them.

○ Step 2

+ Therapist or child will write the affirmation from the cards on a separate piece of paper or index card.

○ Step 3

+ Therapist will direct the child to place the 4 affirmation statements in each of the 4 sections in the sand tray.

○ Step 4

+ Therapist will prompt the child to select one or 2 miniatures for each of their 4 affirmation statements. Engage the child in discussion regarding their tray.

+ Engage the child in identifying challenging thoughts, feelings or activities to which they can apply their positive affirmations outside of the therapy room.

○ Step 5

+ Therapist will ask the child to select one of the affirmations they want to work on during the week. Engage the child in a discussion on how the affirmation will help inspire and motivate them.

+ The client then can report back to the therapist how it was helpful.

+ If the child is not prepared to discuss their tray continue to encourage them to find ways to review the identified affirmations.

+ The therapist takes a picture of the client's affirmation sandtray so that the client and therapist can review the affirmations during future sessions.

Increasing Your Play Therapy Tool Box

Discussion

Affirmations are positive statements that can help you challenge and overcome negative thoughts. When you repeat them often, and believe in them, you can start to make positive changes. Affirmations are a great way for children to practice having a positive mindset daily. It can help them improve their self-esteem and increase their self-confidence.

References:

Manifest Your Magnificence (64 Affirmation Cards for Kids 6-12 Years Old) by Magnificent Creations

Think Before I Speak

Contributed By:Carmen Jimenez-Pride

- ○ Treatment Modality: Individual, Group, Family
- ○ Treatment Phase: Engagement, Working

Materials Needed

1. Thought Worksheet
2. Marker or Crayons
3. Envelope

Goal of the activity

Identifying positive or negative thinking.

Activity Steps

○ **Step 1**

+ Therapist will engage the child in a discussion to identify a positive or negative situation they are involved in or facing.

○ **Step 2**

+ Utilize the thought worksheet and direct the child to identify any positive or negative thoughts they are having about a situation they have identified. Direct the child to write the thoughts in one of the bubbles.

○ **Step 3**

+ Therapist will have a discussion with the child regarding the positive and negative thoughts. Therapist should validate both the positive and negative thoughts the child has identified.

○ **Step 4**

+ Therapist will help the child verbally express their thoughts.

+ When processing thoughts some negative thoughts may need attention and solutions to decrease the power the negative thoughts have over the child.

+ Negative thoughts can be thrown away and positive thoughts can be saved.

Discussion

Often times children have thoughts they do not know how to verbally express or feel that they might get into trouble if they say what is really on their minds. This activity will allow the child to write down their thoughts and share them in an alternative way.

Utilize the envelope to send the negative thoughts away. You can be creative and develop a method send the thoughts away such as a mailbox, a box labeled the thoughts box.

Increasing Your Play Therapy Tool Box

This is my Story

Contributed By: Alisia Mitchell

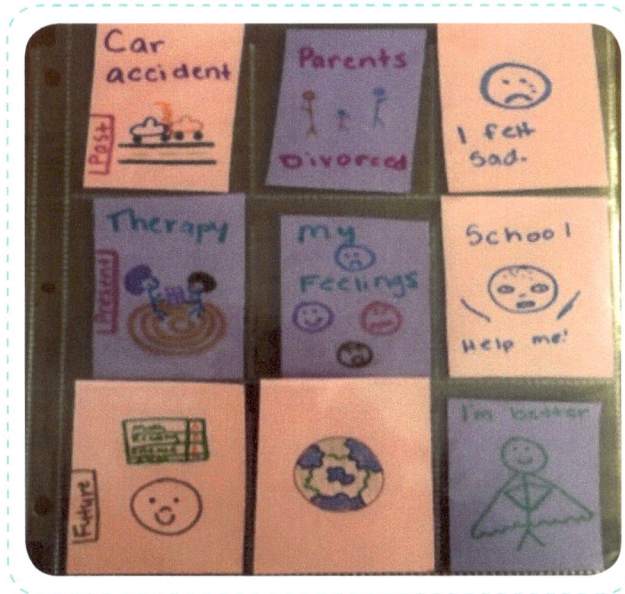

- **Treatment Modality: Individual, Family**
- **Treatment Phase: Working**

Materials Needed

1. **Construction paper**
2. **Markers/colored pencils**
3. **Scissors**
4. **Trading card pages**
5. **Optional:** Magazines or images printed from the Internet and glue

Goal of the activity

To support expressing life events safely and building attachment between client and client/client's parent(s).

Activity Steps

Therapist will prepare before session:

○ Step 1

+ Therapist will cut different colors of construction paper into rectangles to fit inside the trading card pages. It is important to cut between 10-20 rectangles in order for client/client's family to have a variety of colors to select during activity.

**Please note there are 9 open slots for the trading card pages.

○ Step 2

+ Place pre-cut rectangles, the trading card page, and markers/colored pencils aside for client/client's family to use. The rectangles represent a memory or life event about client that client/client's parent will draw/write.

+ Optional: Please note, client/client's parents can also use clippings of magazines or images printed from the internet if desired. Glue will be needed to paste clippings on construction paper.

To begin individual session:

Therapist will introduce session, "We all have memories that are happy, scary, or sad. Memories help us tell our story. Today, we will begin to create your story. Your story can be about your past, present, or future or a special memory for each year you were born." Therapist will direct client to use materials to draw and/or clip images onto construction paper to place inside the slot to illustrate their storyline.

**Therapist will allow client to choose the storyline; such as each slot can be an age of child (first slot-1 years old, second slot-2 years old, etc.), or a specific memory/story, etc.

To start session with client/family:

Therapist will state to family, "We all have memories that are happy, scary, or sad. Memories help us tell our story. Today, we will begin to create your story. Your story can be about your past, present, or future or a special memory for each year you were born. Mom and dad [state caregiver role] can help tell some of your story too." Therapist will direct client to use materials to draw and/or clip images onto construction paper to place inside the slot to illustrate their storyline.

Increasing Your Play Therapy Tool Box

**Therapist will allow client to choose the storyline; such as each slot can be an age of child (first slot-1 years old, second clot-2 years old, etc.), or a specific memory/story, etc.

Discussion

Difficult events in children's lives may be hard to express verbally. This activity was designed in mind for the child who may need support communicating their feelings about past events/memories. The images help the child tell a story that may be uncomfortable, scary, or sad. Additionally, this intervention can assist the parent/parents in communicating safely and connecting with their child in session. With the support of the therapist creating a safe space, the child has an opportunity to express their memories/life events.

Family Crest

Contributed By:Angel Onley-Livingston

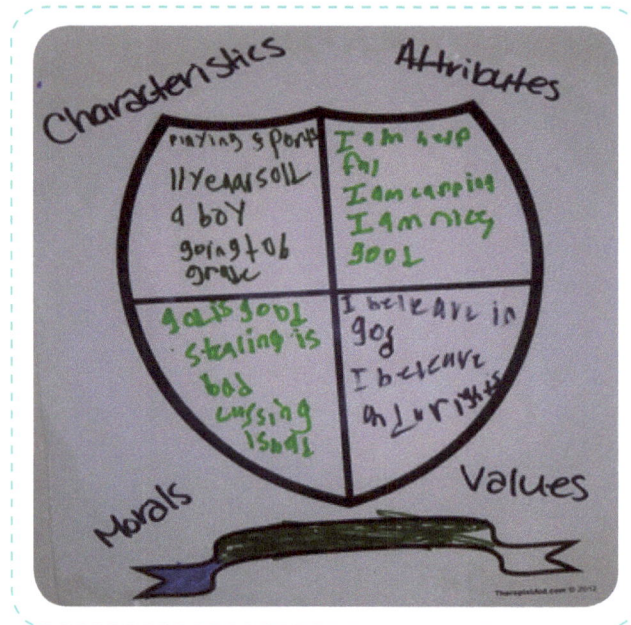

- Treatment Modality: Individual, Group
- Treatment Phase: Working

Materials Needed

1 **Crest Worksheet (Available at Therapy Aid Website)**

2 **Pencil**

3 **Colored Pencils**

4 **Markers**

5 **Crayons**

Goal of the activity

Demonstrate family characteristics, explore sense of self, and explore self-esteem.

Activity Steps

○ Step 1

+ Therapist will explain the meaning of the words morals, values, characteristics, and attributes and engage the child in a discussion to ensure they understand.

○ Step 2

+ Have the child write one of the following in each of the 4 sections of the family crest.

  Section 1: morals, Section 2: values Section 3: characteristics, Section 4: attributes.

○ Step 3

+ Have a suggested list of common norms, values, morals, and attributes for child to pull from in visual form or handout and have child choose 2 to 3 from each list and write them out in each appropriate section. Therapist can pre-fill chart with sections reflected from step 2.

Discussion

What are your personal morals, values, characteristics, and attributes within the family? How does our family view morals, values, characteristics, and attributes? How does it influence who you are?

Negative and Positive Thoughts Memory Game

Contributed By: Sabra Starnes

○ **Treatment Modality: Individual, Group, Family**
○ **Treatment Phase: Working**

Materials Needed

1. **20 Large popsicle sticks**
2. **The Negative and Positive List Word Document**

Goal of the activity

To help the child identify and understand they have both negative and positive thoughts. The child will practice using positive thinking over negative thinking.

Activity Steps

○ Step 1

+ Therapist will lead child in cutting out the positive and negative statements and gluing them to the popsicle sticks.

○ Step 2

+ Before gluing the blank positive and negative, have the child identify and write their own positive and negative thought then glue it to the sticks.

○ Step 3

+ Therapist will turn popsicle sticks upside down and mix the popsicle sticks around so that they are separated.

+ The game is played like the memory game.

+ Once all the popsicle sticks are mixed up and face down the game can begin.

+ The child goes first, and turns over 2 popsicle sticks to search for a positive statement that will change the negative statement.

+ When all the negative and positive pairs are collected by the client and the therapist. Each count their pairs; the winner is with the person with the most pairs.

○ Step 4

+ Therapist assist the child with choosing one negative thought that they want to work on during the week. They can choose to pick from either their pile or the therapist pile. The therapist and child together identify and address how the child can practice using the positive thought instead of the negative thought.

Discussion

Let children know that we all have both negative and positive thoughts about situations in our lives. Talking with the child about how we can change our negative thoughts to positive thoughts to help us feel happier and less stressed. Also, the change will help us be able to cope with conflict and problematic situation in a healthier manner. This activity will help children to see that they can be more in charge of changing their thoughts and that their thoughts do not have to become facts.

NEGATIVE THOUGHTS	POSITIVE THOUGHTS
I am not a good person	I am not a good person
I never do anything right	I can try and do things right
Others don't like me	People like me for who I am
I always make mistakes	I can learn from my mistakes and do better
Nothing ever good happens to me	Good things do and can happen for me
I am not loveable person	I am a love able person
"This is all my fault"	It is not always my fault
I am weak person and won't be able to do the things I want to do in life.	I am a strong person That can do the things that Iwant to do in life
I quit, because I never win	I am not going to give up, even if I win or lose.
I can't trust myself or anyone else	I can trust myself and others
I have to lie to others and to myself	I can be honest with others and myself

End of the Rainbow

Contributed By:Carmen Jimenez-Pride

○ **Treatment Modality: Individual, Group, Family**
○ **Treatment Phase: Termination**

Materials Needed

1 **End of the Rainbow worksheet**
2 **Crayons or Markers**

Goal of the activity

Outlining goals achieved during treatment or skills learned.

Activity Steps

○ **Step 1**

+ Therapist and child will discuss what lead them to therapy and write it in the cloud.

○ **Step 2**

+ Therapist will lead the child in identifying a goal they set at the beginning of the therapeutic process, write it in the pot.

○ **Step 3**

+ Within the lines of the rainbow identify coping skills, changes and thoughts that helped them reach their goals.

Discussion

This activity also can be used towards the end of the therapeutic relationship to outline the progress that was made while in treatment. This will allow the child to see the progress they have made during the course of treatment. Of course, this is an opportunity for the child to be creative. The worksheet can be used to identify positive affirmations during an individual session or family session.

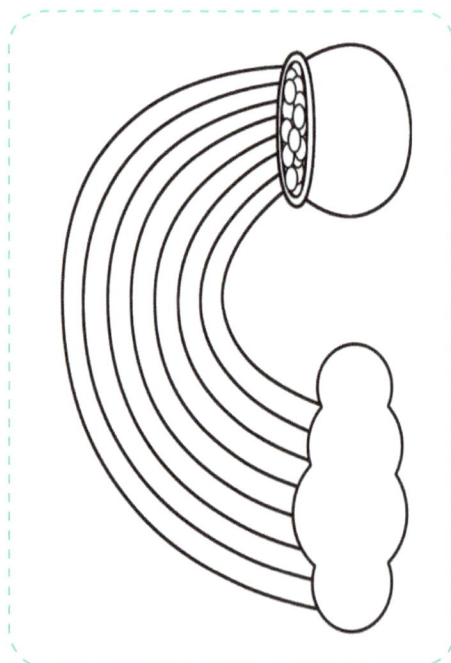

Increasing Your Play Therapy Tool Box

Personal Crest Collage

Contributed By: Angel Onley-Livingston

- ° **Treatment Modality: Individual, Group**
- ° **Treatment Phase: Working, Termination**

Materials Needed

1. **Crest Worksheet** (Available at Therapy Aid Website) https://www.therapistaid.com/worksheets/coat-of-arms-family-crest.pdf
2. **Pencils**
3. **Colored Pencils**
4. **Markers**
5. **Crayons**
6. **Scissors**
7. **Glue Stick**
8. **4 or 5 Magazines**
9. **1 Poster board half size**

Goal of the activity

To demonstrate personal strength characteristics, and attributes. To demonstrate positive personal traits. To discuss personal morals. To explore sense of self. To discuss and explore self-esteem.

○ **Step 1**

+ Therapist will explain the definition of morals, values, characteristics, and attributes.

○ **Step 2**

+ Have the child write in each of the four sections: section 1: personal section 2: morals section.

○ **Step 3**

+ Allow 10 to 15 minutes for child to cut out pictures from magazines that represent role models, images, or words that represents their morals, values, characteristics, and attributes.

○ **Step 4**

+ Direct the child, with therapist help if needed, glue pictures onto the poster board provided in any position the child wishes. Have the child verbally explain and process what they now know about themselves through their visual representation of self in their crest.

Discussion

Discuss the following with the child:

1. Chosen personal attributes.

2. Discuss personal morals.

3. Discuss personal characteristics.

4. Discuss personal traits.

5. Discuss how attributes, morals, traits, and characteristics represent who they are?

6. How does their personal crest define them as an individual?

7. How do they define self-awareness through their personal crest?

Doll Making Activity

Contributed By: Angel Onley-Livingston

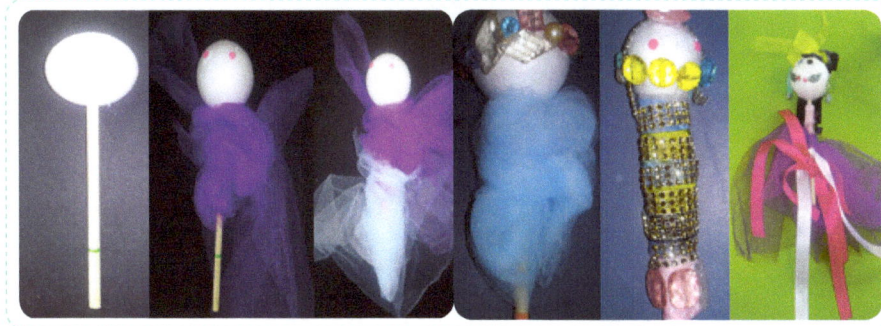

- Treatment Modality: Individual, Group, Family
- Treatment Phase: Working

Materials Needed

1. **1 Styrofoam ball per person 2 to 3-inch diameter**
2. **Mesh (assorted colors half a foot strips)**
3. **Decorative stones and gems in a bin or containers presorted to choose from**
4. **Wood sticks 6 to 12 inches in length 1 per person**
5. **Hot glue gun (supervision always) 1 per every 3 persons**
6. **Hot glue sticks at least 3 per person per gun**
7. **Strips of colored fabric material, rectangle or square shaped. 6 inches on all sides.**
8. **Assortment of ribbon to tie and gather mesh and materials**

Goal of the activity

To create a doll that represents child's personal self or current journey of self-discovery. To demonstrate evolving, learning, changing, growth in therapy, goals, self-actualization and identity.

Activity Steps

1. Therapist will direct child to push wooden stick into the Styrofoam ball half way through.

2. Direct child to pull out the stick and add drop of glue in the hole.

3. Direct child push stick back in to secure the doll head.

4. Allow child to choose two pieces of mesh and two pieces of material to make the body of the doll.

5. Direct child to bunch and wrap mesh and secure it on the stick with hot glue and ribbon of their choice

6. Direct child to bundle mesh at the top to be the bust/torso of doll and bottom bundle will be legs skirt/kilt or draping.

7. Direct child to decorate with ribbon and decorative gems with supervision to show their unique personality and evolvement in therapy or in life. With smaller children let them hand you the objects and you secure and place objects on the doll.

8. Once the doll is complete allow the child to verbally process and discuss the colors and gems chosen to represent their doll.

9. Direct child to write using narrative therapy a reflective writing about their experience in the process of creating the doll. Have them write about their difficulties and or ease, and how this shows up in their life. This journal entry can be used in the group discussion below to help child process what to say in the circle or group.

Discussion

Discussion is done in a group or individual format. Discuss progression and regression in therapy for each child. How does the child think therapy and life is going since they have been in therapy for about 6 weeks to 2 months? Review with child their progress and regression. Allow child to do the same while creating the doll to represent this as well. Discuss current setbacks and/or weaknesses that inhibit their growth and changes in their therapeutic process.

Increasing Your Play Therapy Tool Box